ALICE'S COOKBOOK

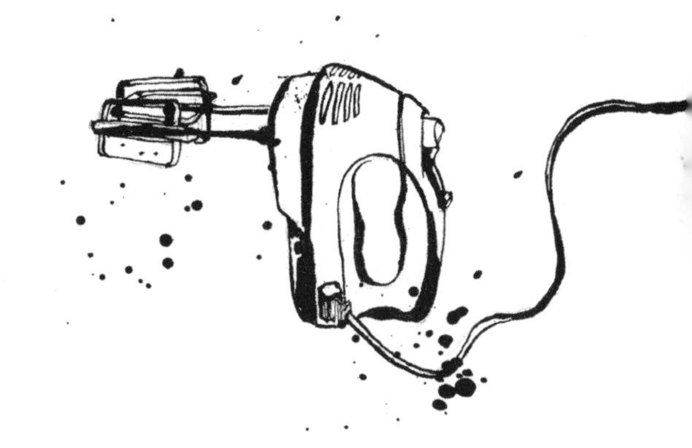

LYONS PRESS
Guilford, Connecticut
An imprint of Globe Pequot Press

★

alice's COOK BOOK

ALICE HART

Photography by Emma Lee
Illustrations by Ruth Jackson

For my mum, Jasmine

First published in 2010 by
Quadrille Publishing Limited

First Lyons Press edition 2011

Lyons Press is an imprint of Globe Pequot Press

Library of Congress Cataloging-in-Publication Data is available on file.

ISBN 978-0-7627-7018-2

Printed in China

10 9 8 7 6 5 4 3 2 1

Quadrille Publishing Limited
Alhambra House
27-31 Charing Cross Road
London WC2H 0LS
www.quadrille.co.uk

EDITORIAL DIRECTOR Anne Furniss
CREATIVE DIRECTOR Helen Lewis
PROJECT EDITOR Lucy Bannell
EDITOR U.S. EDITION Norma MacMillan
DESIGNER Claire Peters
PHOTOGRAPHER Emma Lee
ILLUSTRATOR Ruth Jackson
STYLIST Tabitha Hawkins
PRODUCTION DIRECTOR Vincent Smith
PRODUCTION CONTROLLER Ruth Deary

The Penguin Book of English Verse
INTRODUCED AND EDITED BY JOHN HAYWARD

It is the feasts enjoyed with friends and family that are always the most fondly remembered. Food eaten at leisure, and in celebration, is the backbone of my cooking and it's become second nature to prepare it without fuss. That's what I want to pass on to you: my strategies for spending time in the kitchen intelligently and enjoyably so that you can feed any number as serenely as possible, because I understand what it's like to have little precious free time.

I'm not really a pre-prepared food or quick-fix kind of girl. But please don't see that as a snobbish statement. Like you, I have a busy life to lead and am far from a Stepford type. Admittedly, cooking is a priority and a joy for me, but I'd rather spend time making a marinade or cake a day or two before the main event to free up time later. From Sunday lunches to cocktail parties to picnics, some preparation time snatched here and there saves getting flustered on the day. The very idea of chopping madly at the last minute, as the doorbell rings, fills me with horror. I love having friends over, feeding them, cooking for them... Why would I want to make it a torture? When lunch is pretty much in the bag, life is more relaxed (and we can all go outside and enjoy the sunshine). This advance prepping is my way of picking a path through life's vicissitudes, with sanity somewhat intact and delectable food on the table.

Deciding what to cook, for any number, can take practice. Each menu in this book has been carefully thought through to make it as seamless as possible, and a couple of the more involved meals even contain a time plan to help with the logistics. Oven temperatures have been synced wherever they can be, and last-minute preparation kept to a minimum. Of course, you don't have to cook an entire menu: the individual recipes will stand proudly alone.

While I hesitate to quote dictatorial rules, there are a few that apply to food (to be broken as you wish). Try to introduce contrasts: rich with light; bite with soft; fried with steamed. And, in general, keep to one country or area to avoid muddying flavors: for example, a Thai curry is best with simply steamed rice, rather than a Persian pilaf.

There are lines to be drawn, I feel, when writing and following recipes. Certain detail is, of course, good and necessary—pan size, cooking time, and the like—but too much can be obtrusive and quashes natural instinct. My intent is to encourage you to enjoy cooking well and to nurture the appreciation of food it brings. How you get there in your own kitchen will be affected by so many factors; I'm merely here to guide, without smothering or bombarding. So beyond the realms of precise baking measurements and oven temperatures, do what feels right—add more chile if you crave heat, or use maple syrup in place of honey. These are your recipes now.

I see a healthy dose of pride and enthusiasm for cooking, particularly among my contemporaries, with other, more exotic, cuisines being happily embraced. With today's horizons broader than ever, our kitchens sing with new flavors. Each place I visit has had an impact on my cooking, be it an animated corner of an Italian cafe or an Indian tea house. You'll find a few Vietnamese, Thai, Italian, Moroccan, and Indian-influenced recipes peppered throughout this book, because those cuisines inspire me. But the basis for my cooking is close to home, which for me is Great Britain.

These menus are seasonal, but can be easily adapted to use the produce that is best in the month during which you are cooking. Substitute like for like—leaf for leaf or root for root—and problems will be unlikely. Seasonal eating is important not merely because of the superior taste of produce at its peak, but because it is an economical way to dine—a way to avoid compromise by buying when abundance forces prices down.

This isn't principally a book of everyday food, though you will find many simple ideas for lunch and supper, but I hope you'll invent reasons to celebrate and to cook from it often. That's the point: the recipes are meant to make dinners, parties, or camping expeditions both more enjoyable and more achievable. Corny it may be, but love, laughter, and eating well are bound together and that should always be so.

"It is more fun to talk with someone who doesn't use long, difficult words but rather short, easy words like 'What about lunch?' "

WINNIE THE POOH
FROM THE HOUSE AT POOH CORNER BY A. A. MILNE

★

BREAKFAST AND BRUNCH

FROM A HASTILY EATEN MUFFIN TO A LEISURELY BRUNCH STRETCHING LUNCHWARDS, THE FIRST FUEL OF THE DAY HAS MORE IMPORTANCE THAN MOST OF US ASCRIBE TO IT. BE THAT AS IT MAY, IN MY EXPERIENCE A LOVINGLY PREPARED BREAKFAST USUALLY COMES SECOND BEST TO SLEEPING, JOGGING, OR WHATEVER ELSE YOU CHOOSE TO DO WITH YOUR EARLY MORNINGS. BY DOING A BIT OF PREP THE NIGHT BEFORE YOU'LL FIND IT EASY TO ACHIEVE, EVEN IF YOU ARE FEEDING LARGER NUMBERS.

EASY, PORTABLE BREAKFAST FOR A CROWD OF EIGHT

Apple and Almond Muesli

Boursin Omelet Baguettes

Honey's Raspberry Turnovers

Destined for autumn, this is a weekend feast to lay out on the table and leave there until you have a full house. Sometimes, getting everybody up at the same time, let alone sitting around a table, is too much to ask. None of these recipes will mind waiting around until an owner scoops them up. They'll need lots of hot coffee, tea, or juice to go with them. For stragglers, much of breakfast is portable—perfect for eating on the run if you have somewhere to go in a rush.

APPLE AND ALMOND MUESLI

HANDS-ON TIME: 15 MINUTES

FOR THE MUESLI
4 cups rolled oats
1½ cups apple cider
⅔ cup milk or water
¾–1 cup chopped unblanched almonds or sliced almonds
3 apples

FOR SERVING
Milk
Thick, plain yogurt
¼ cup mixed seeds (sunflower, sesame, pumpkin)
Seasonal berries or extra chopped apple
Mild honey

This muesli is an embarrassingly easy recipe that still manages to impress everyone. It is always especially popular with healthy-living types. Vary the components as you like, but keep the basic oat-to-liquid ratio the same. A bowl of the soaked oats and fruit juice mixture will keep in the refrigerator for several days, ready to be further customized with extra fruit, nuts, seeds, yogurt, and milk.

The night before, or at least a couple of hours before you want to eat, mix the oats, apple cider, and milk or water with half the almonds in a large bowl. Cover with a plate and refrigerate.

When you're ready for breakfast, coarsely grate the apples, avoiding the cores, and fold into the oat mixture. Let everyone construct his or her own bowl of muesli, adding milk and/or yogurt, a spoonful of the remaining almonds, seeds, berries or apple, and honey to sweeten.

HONEY'S RASPBERRY TURNOVERS

HANDS-ON TIME: 15 MINUTES

Flour, for dusting
1 pound puff pastry, preferably made with butter, thawed if frozen
4 heaping cups fresh raspberries
About ½ cup plain or vanilla-flavored sugar
1 free-range egg yolk, mixed with 1 tablespoon milk

Honey, my baker-extraordinaire, puff-pastry-making grandmother, has been an expert with a turnover for as long as I can remember, churning out batches of apple, apricot, or raspberry from a handsome blue stove. Try to use all-butter puff pastry: it tastes so much better than pastry made with vegetable fat.

On a lightly floured surface, roll out the pastry to form a ½-inch-thick rectangle. Use a sharp knife to trim the raggedy edges straight, then cut into eight even squares. They should each be about 6 x 6 inches.

Place a pile of raspberries on each square, slightly off-center, and add a heaping teaspoon of sugar. With a pastry brush, paint a little water around the edge and bring one corner over to meet its diagonal opposite. Press the edges together firmly to seal, using the tines of a fork if you like. Repeat to make a total of eight pastries, spacing them out on a baking sheet. At this stage, the turnovers can be refrigerated for up to 2 days.

Preheat the oven to 400°F. Brush the pastry surfaces with the egg wash (yolk and milk mixture) and sprinkle with a little more sugar. Cut a small vent in the top of each to let the steam out, then bake until plump and golden, about 20 minutes. Let cool for a while on a wire rack and serve warm.

BOURSIN OMELET BAGUETTES won't mind sitting around for a bit at room temperature, ready to be re-warmed in a low oven when any stragglers find their way to the kitchen. Make two at a time. Warm a couple of lengths of very fresh French bread in the oven. Meanwhile, beat three or four free-range eggs lightly in a bowl. Add just a little seasoning and a couple of tablespoons of coarsely crumbled Boursin (garlic and herb) soft cheese. Melt a pat of butter in a frying pan and, when foaming, tip in your eggs, shaking the pan as they hit the hot butter. As the egg cooks, draw it in from the edges with a spoon or spatula and tilt the pan to allow the raw egg to run into the space. When almost cooked, but still a little runny, split the warmed bread and spread with butter and more Boursin. Fold the omelet over and tip out of the pan. Cut in half and stuff into the baguettes. Add a few halved cherry tomatoes and/or a handful of peppery arugula leaves, if you like, then enjoy.

NEW YEAR BRUNCH FOR EIGHT

Crisp, Maple-Sugared Bacon with
Oven Hash Browns and Poached Eggs

Baked Beans

Orchard Pastries

Mocha Affogatos

Pomegranate Fizz

Unless you like cooking on a snatched few hours of sleep, this is probably best for a civilized New Year's Day, or at least for a late brunch. That's not to say it's difficult: there are a few tricks tucked in the methods to make life easier. Check in advance for any non-meat eaters so you can make the veggie version of the beans to keep everyone happy.

CRISP, MAPLE-SUGARED BACON WITH OVEN HASH BROWNS AND POACHED EGGS

HANDS-ON TIME: 15 MINUTES

FOR THE HASH BROWNS
2 large baking potatoes
2 large sweet potatoes
1 small onion, finely sliced
Small bunch of chives, snipped
6 tablespoons olive oil
Salt and pepper

FOR THE BACON
16 medium or thick bacon slices
3 tablespoons maple syrup
Pinch of cayenne

FOR SERVING
8 very fresh free-range eggs
Easy Tomato, Bell Pepper, and Chile Jam (see page 32)

As someone who can even burn toast with frustrating regularity, I have learned that gentle oven-cooking of bacon is far less risky than broiling. And cooking hash browns in the oven is foolproof. There are lots of tricks for poaching eggs. I find vinegar in the water produces vinegary egg whites, while whirling vortexes in the pan aren't much use when you're cooking eight eggs. The very best advice I can offer is to use the freshest eggs you can find.

Preheat the oven to 350°F. Peel the baking and sweet potatoes and grate coarsely. Pile into a clean dish towel with the onion, twist into a log shape, and wring hard to squeeze out excess liquid. Shake into a bowl and add the chives, half the oil, and plenty of seasoning. Generously oil two 12-cup muffin pans and flatten a tight-packed ball of potato into each cup (or you can cook the patties on a large baking sheet, spacing well apart). Bake until golden and toasted at the edges, about 40 minutes.

Gently toss the bacon with the syrup and cayenne in a bowl, then lay out on a baking sheet. Cook in the oven with the hash browns until dark golden and crisp, 25–30 minutes, turning over halfway.

About 10 minutes before the hash browns are done, fill a large, deep-sided frying pan with water and bring to simmering point; the water should be barely bubbling. Crack an egg into a teacup and very carefully slide it into the water. Repeat with the remaining eggs. Cook until the whites are just set, about 3 minutes. Scoop out with a slotted spoon and drain on a plate lined with paper towels.

Serve the eggs, hash browns, and bacon with a dollop of Easy Tomato, Bell Pepper, and Chile Jam (see page 32). Good old ketchup makes a winning accompaniment, too.

BAKED BEANS

HANDS-ON TIME: 15 MINUTES

- 1 pound dried cranberry beans (about 3 cups)
- 2 tablespoons dark brown sugar, preferably Muscovado sugar
- 1 heaping teaspoon English mustard powder, or for a milder flavor use yellow mustard powder
- 1 onion, chopped
- 1 14-ounce can crushed tomatoes
- 1 rosemary sprig
- 1 small, smoked ham hock (optional)
- Salt and pepper

A misleading title, because these beans aren't baked. To cut down the prep time you can use four 14-ounce cans of beans, well drained, instead of soaking and cooking dried beans. The smoked ham hock gives wonderful flavor, but if you'd rather keep the beans vegetarian, replace it with a few sun-dried tomatoes and 1 teaspoon smoked paprika. The beans will keep in the refrigerator for at least a week.

Soak the dried beans for at least 8 hours, or overnight, in plenty of cold water. (If you forget, or don't have time for such a long soaking, cover them with cold water in a large saucepan, bring to a boil, and simmer briskly for a few minutes before setting aside to soak for 1–2 hours.) Drain the beans, cover with fresh water, and bring to a rolling boil. Simmer until just tender, about 1 hour. Drain, but reserve the cooking water.

Mix the cooked (or canned) beans with the remaining ingredients in a large saucepan and cover with 2 cups of the reserved cooking liquid (or with water if you're using canned beans). Cover the pan, then simmer very gently until completely tender, about 1 hour. If you used it, fish out the ham hock and cut the meat into small pieces, discarding bone, fat, and gristle. Return the meat to the beans and season to taste with pepper and a little salt.

ORCHARD PASTRIES

HANDS-ON TIME: 20 MINUTES

- 12 ounces puff pastry, preferably made with butter, thawed if frozen, or double quantity Quick Flaky Pastry recipe (see page 78)
- Flour, for dusting
- 1 free-range egg
- 2 tablespoons light brown sugar
- 2 tablespoons cream cheese
- 1 tablespoon ground almonds
- ½ teaspoon ground cinnamon
- 1 apple, quartered, cored, and thinly sliced
- 1 ripe pear, quartered, cored, and sliced
- Milk
- 2 tablespoons warmed apricot jam

Ripe plums, apricots, or peaches make lovely stand-ins for these pears and apples during the warmer months. Just use whatever's good and seasonal.

Roll out the puff pastry or Quick Flaky Pastry on a lightly floured surface and cut into eight squares, each about 5 x 5 inches. Preheat the oven to 350°F.

Beat the egg, sugar, cream cheese, almonds, and cinnamon together. Spoon a dollop into the center of each pastry square. Top with sliced apple or pear, fanning the pieces out slightly. Pinch two diagonal pastry corners together and dab with milk to seal (the resulting pastry shape should be a square with pointy ends). Brush the pastry surface with a little more milk.

Place on a large baking sheet, well spaced, and bake until the pastry is golden, about 15 minutes. Cool on the baking sheet for 5 minutes before moving the pastries to a wire rack. Spread a little jam over the fruit, using the back of a teaspoon, then eat warm or let cool.

MOCHA AFFOGATOS

HANDS-ON TIME: 10 MINUTES

- 8 small scoops chocolate ice cream
- 1 cup hot, freshly brewed, strong espresso
- 2 ounces bittersweet chocolate, coarsely grated

Affogatos are traditionally enjoyed later in the day, though I don't see why they shouldn't make a chic appearance at brunch. Give in to the allure of the morning gelato! Use vanilla ice cream if chocolate seems too much. There's nowhere for the ingredients to hide, so use the very best quality ice cream, coffee, and chocolate possible.

Divide the ice cream among eight small heatproof glasses or cups. Top each scoop with a dash of espresso and sprinkle with a little grated chocolate. Serve immediately, with teaspoons, before too much melting occurs.

A decadent **POMEGRANATE FIZZ** should complement all things brunch. Squeeze the juice from 1 large or 2 small pomegranates. The easiest way to do this is to halve the fruit and crush/squeeze the juice into a bowl just as you would a lemon. Strain the juice into a pitcher because it's bound to have stray seeds and bits of pith in it. Divide the juice among eight champagne glasses and fill them up with chilled champagne, prosecco, or dry sparkling white wine.

Ficelle
Koord

BUTTERY APPLE, HONEY, AND POLENTA LOAF CAKE

SERVES 8-10
HANDS-ON TIME: 20 MINUTES

A simple, rustic cake for a crowd, this has a light, lemony syrup poured over as it cools. My grandparents have kept bees for more than 50 years and, although they can't do the work themselves any more, the hives are still in use. The gently flavored honey their bees make is perfect for this cake, although any mild honey would work well, either whipped or regular.

FOR THE CAKE

1 cup (2 sticks) unsalted butter, softened
⅔ cup whipped honey
3 extra-large free-range eggs
1 cup ground almonds
1 cup all-purpose flour
1 cup polenta
Finely grated zest of 2 lemons
Juice of 1 lemon
2 apples, quartered, cored, and chopped small
1 teaspoon baking powder
½ teaspoon salt

FOR THE GLAZE

3 tablespoons whipped honey
Juice of 1 lemon

Line a 4½ x 8½-inch loaf pan with parchment paper. Preheat the oven to 350°F.

Beat the butter and honey together until light and fluffy. Add the eggs, one at a time, beating well between each addition to make the batter light, then fold in the remaining cake ingredients. Spoon into the pan and level the top with the back of a spoon. Bake until well risen and golden, about 1 hour.

Unmold onto a wire rack, right side up, and pierce all over with a skewer. To make the glaze, gently heat the honey in a small pan and stir in the lemon juice. Let cool for a couple of minutes. Place a plate under the cake to catch the run-off and spoon the warm glaze over the cake. Serve warm or cool, as it is, or with plain yogurt and/or apple compote for brunch.

SPRING BREAKFAST FOR SIX ON THE WEEKEND
(TO MAKE THE NIGHT BEFORE)

Maple and Blueberry Sticky Rolls

Tropical Fruit Platter with Kaffir Lime

Sunshine Juice

The smell of yeasty, syrup-spiked dough baking could sell any house in the land. If you make and knead the dough the night before, you too can have a kitchen as fragrantly delicious as a bakery (and all will marvel at your genius). Make the fruit salad beforehand too and refrigerate. The juice only takes a very few minutes in the morning.

TROPICAL FRUIT PLATTER WITH KAFFIR LIME

HANDS-ON TIME: 20 MINUTES

- ¼ cup sugar
- 2 small kaffir lime leaves, finely sliced (or the finely grated zest of 1 lime)
- Juice of 2 limes
- 2 ripe mangoes
- 1 ripe pineapple, peeled, cored, and chopped into wedges
- 1 fat wedge from a watermelon, skin removed and flesh sliced
- 1 ripe papaya, peeled, halved, deseeded, and sliced
- 12 fresh lychees, peeled and pitted, or 1 14-ounce can lychees, drained

It almost goes without saying that the fruit can be varied according to whim or weather. Just choose the sweetest and ripest you can find.

Gently heat the sugar with ¼ cup water until it dissolves. Bring to a boil, then remove from the heat and add the lime leaves (or lime zest) and lime juice. Set aside.

To prepare the mango, cut the fat cheeks from either side of the flat pit. Score the flesh in a criss-cross pattern and turn the skin "inside out" so that the mango flesh sticks out like cuboid spikes. Cut the cubes off the skin.

Arrange all the fruit on a serving plate and spoon the kaffir lime syrup over. Cover and chill for at least 1 hour, or up to 8 hours, to infuse the fruit with the kaffir lime perfume.

MAPLE AND BLUEBERRY STICKY ROLLS

HANDS-ON TIME: 30 MINUTES

FOR THE MAPLE BUTTER

- ⅔ cup unsalted butter, softened
- ½ cup maple syrup
- ¾ cup packed light brown sugar

FOR THE BUNS

- 1½ cups milk
- ¼ cup (½ stick) unsalted butter, plus more for the pan
- 2 tablespoons active dry yeast, or 1 tablespoon quick-rising dry yeast
- 6 tablespoons light brown sugar
- 2½ cups all-purpose flour, plus more for dusting
- 1 teaspoon salt
- 1 cup dried blueberries
- 3 tablespoons maple syrup

If you want to bake a batch of sticky rolls in the morning, let the dough rise in the refrigerator overnight, then shape and bake the next day. This makes 12 rolls, but I don't think that will be too many...

Start with the maple butter. Beat the butter, syrup, and sugar together until light. Set aside at room temperature, or refrigerate if not using until the next day.

For the buns, heat the milk and, just before it boils, add the butter. Set aside until cooled to body temperature.

Meanwhile, put ½ cup warm water in a small measuring cup. Stir in the yeast and a large pinch of the sugar. Leave it in a warm place to activate for 5 minutes or so; the yeast should bubble up to form a lovely frothy top.

Place all the remaining sugar, the flour, and salt in a large bowl and make a well in the center. Add the activated yeast and the buttery milk and bring together with your hands to form a dough. Knead on a floured surface until the dough is silky-smooth and elastic, 8–10 minutes, then transfer to an oiled bowl. (Or let a mixer take the strain; the kneading will only take 5 minutes.)

Cover the bowl with oiled plastic wrap and let rise in a warm place for 1 hour. (If you let it rise in the refrigerator overnight, bring it to room temperature before proceeding with the recipe.)

Preheat the oven to 400°F. Give the risen dough a satisfying punch, then dust with flour and knead it for a minute. Roll and stretch out to form a large rectangle (about 10 x 16 inches). Spread two-thirds of the maple butter over the dough and sprinkle with the dried blueberries. Fold in one long edge by one-third, then fold the other long edge third over this, as if you were folding a letter to put in an envelope. Now gently roll out the dough to a large rectangle as before and spread with the remaining maple butter. This time, roll up from a long edge to form a log shape.

Cut the log into 12 equal pieces that will look like pinwheels. Butter a 12-cup muffin pan and place a piece of dough, cut side up, in each cup. Let rise in a warm place for 10 minutes, then drizzle with the maple syrup and bake for 30 minutes. Carefully remove the rolls from the muffin pan while hot, or they'll stick, but let them cool a little before eating.

Been overdoing the parties and the sticky rolls? If you have, a **SUNSHINE JUICE** should begin to sort things out... You'll need a juicer to make this (or just mix fresh apple, orange, and carrot juices in a pitcher with strained fresh ginger pulp and ice cubes). For each serving, juice 2 carrots, 1 apple, 1 large orange, and half a thumb-size piece of fresh ginger. Stir well, add ice, and serve as soon as possible to get the best out of the vitamins.

SUMMER BRUNCH FOR 12

Baked Pistachio Granola,
Apricot Compote, and Yogurt

Sugared Brioche Perdu with
Crushed Strawberries

Brunch Frittata with Easy Tomato,
Bell Pepper, and Chile Jam

Cheddar Cornbread Muffins

Mango Lassi

Iced Coffee

Twelve is a good number for brunch and conversation, but not such a good number to cook complicated, individual egg orders for. So I suggest a menu of good-natured beauties, all placid enough to sit around for a while. And they won't be much trouble to get together in the first place. Any minutes you can spare the day before will put you ahead, come the morning.

MANGO LASSI

HANDS-ON TIME: 15 MINUTES

- 3 large and ripe, fragrant mangoes, or 2½ cups canned mango puree
- 2½ cups thick, plain yogurt
- 2½ cups chilled water
- 3 handfuls of crushed ice
- Sugar or mild honey, to taste (optional)

On hot days, this cooling Indian drink is incredibly refreshing. If you'd prefer something salty (which is much nicer than it sounds), leave out the mango and sugar or honey, and replace them with a pinch each of toasted cumin seeds and salt. You can also add a touch of grated fresh ginger to the sweet or salty versions before blending.

Peel and pit the mangoes, then roughly chop the flesh.

Pulse one-third of the mango flesh with one-third of the yogurt, water, and ice in a blender until smooth, then taste and decide if it's sweet enough for you. If not, add a little sugar or honey and blend again. Divide among four glasses. Repeat twice more to fill another eight glasses.

Making **ICED COFFEE** the night before is so easy, and a cold drink is perfect on a hot summer's day. You can also make the coffee really strong, and then dilute it with milk or ice water for those of more delicate constitutions. Measure 2 tablespoons coffee and ½ cup of water per person into a large pitcher. Stir well and refrigerate overnight. The next morning, add another ½ cup of chilled water per person, stir again, and strain through a fine sieve or coffee filter paper. Serve the chilled coffee over ice, black or topped with chilled milk, and sweetened with sugar to taste.

BAKED PISTACHIO GRANOLA, APRICOT COMPOTE, AND YOGURT

HANDS-ON TIME: 25 MINUTES

FOR THE GRANOLA

- 1 large, tart apple, peeled, cored, and chopped
- 1 cup maple syrup
- 7½ cups oats (see right)
- ½ cup each pumpkin, sunflower, and sesame seeds
- ½ cup roughly chopped unsalted pistachios
- 2 tablespoons walnut, almond, or mild olive oil
- ½ teaspoon ground cinnamon
- 2 cups dried apricots, snipped into pieces

FOR THE COMPOTE

- 1 vanilla bean, split lengthwise
- 18 small, ripe apricots, halved and pitted
- ½ cup maple syrup

FOR SERVING

- Ice-cold milk or plain yogurt

Which genius came up with the idea of eating oatmeal cookies with milk for breakfast? That's basically what the more sugary, fatty granolas are. Making your own cereal allows you to tweak the oil and sugar levels, resulting in a vastly superior granola. When it comes to oats, play around and see what you like best. I tend to use two-thirds Scottish (steel-cut) oats and one-third rolled oats or oatmeal for the robust texture I prefer. Any leftover granola can be kept in an airtight container. It will become worryingly addictive once you know it's there.

Start with a quick applesauce for the granola. Gently simmer the chopped apple in a covered saucepan with a splash of water until the apple breaks down, about 10 minutes. Stir in 2 tablespoons of the syrup.

Preheat the oven to 325°F. Combine the applesauce with the oats, seeds, nuts, oil, cinnamon, and rest of the syrup. Spread out on a large baking sheet lined with parchment paper. Bake for 25 minutes, stirring every 10 minutes or so to make sure it browns evenly. Add the apricots and bake for 10–15 minutes longer. Do keep an eye on it and reduce the heat if it browns too quickly. Cool the granola on the sheet, then use right away, or store in an airtight container in a cool, dark place for up to 3 weeks. If the oats start to go soft, refresh the granola by giving it a blast in a hot oven to re-crisp.

To make the compote, scrape the seeds from the vanilla bean with the tip of a knife. Heat the apricots with the syrup, vanilla bean, and seeds in a small pan over gentle heat until soft, about 10 minutes. Stir now and then, but remove from the heat before the apricots start to lose their shape. Let cool, then fish out the vanilla bean. Serve the compote with the cold cereal and milk or yogurt.

EASY TOMATO, BELL PEPPER, AND CHILE JAM

MAKES 3 JARS
HANDS-ON TIME: 15 MINUTES

- 2 fat garlic cloves, peeled
- 3 long, red chiles (medium or hot)
- 1-ounce piece fresh ginger, peeled
- 12 ounces ripe tomatoes
- 2 red bell peppers, deseeded
- ¾ cup Demerara sugar
- ½ teaspoon salt, or 1 tablespoon fish sauce
- ¼ cup rice vinegar

This sweet-hot jam will lift any savory breakfast dish. It is particularly wonderful with herby, baked ricotta. Make it in late summer, when tomatoes, bell peppers, and chiles are at their best.

Pulse the garlic, chiles, and fresh ginger in a mini food processor until minced.

Chop the tomatoes roughly and the bell peppers a little more finely. Put everything in a large saucepan with the sugar, salt or fish sauce, and vinegar.

Bring to a boil and simmer, stirring often, until reduced and viscous, about 30 minutes. Ladle into warm, sterilized jars (see page 89), screw on the lids tightly, and turn upside down to cool. Keep in the refrigerator and use within 4 months.

BRUNCH FRITTATA WITH EASY TOMATO, BELL PEPPER, AND CHILE JAM

HANDS-ON TIME: 25 MINUTES

8 fresh pork link sausages
2 red bell peppers, deseeded and thickly sliced
Olive oil
1 large bunch of scallions, trimmed and sliced
2 cups sliced mushrooms
1 garlic clove, minced
Small handful of cilantro or parsley leaves, chopped
Salt and pepper
4 teaspoons Easy Tomato, Bell Pepper, and Chile Jam (see page 32), plus more for serving
2 tablespoons Greek yogurt or crème fraîche
6 extra-large free-range eggs, lightly beaten

Don't feel constrained by the word brunch *in the title: breakfast, lunch, or supper are all eminently suitable occasions for a hearty frittata. If you do not want to make your own jam, you can use a purchased chile jam or relish.*

Preheat the broiler. Toss the sausages and bell peppers with a little olive oil, then broil until the sausages are cooked, about 10 minutes, turning frequently. Any blackening of the peppers is nothing to worry about. Set aside to cool slightly, then chop the sausages into large chunks. Leave the broiler on.

In a very large frying pan (about 12 inches diameter), fry the scallions in a little oil for 2 minutes. Add the mushrooms and garlic and sauté for 5–7 minutes longer. Stir in the herbs, peppers, and sausages, distributing everything evenly. Season well and spoon dollops of the Chile Jam and yogurt around the pan.

Carefully pour in the eggs. Cook over a medium-low heat for 10 minutes, then place the pan under the broiler and cook until the frittata is just set on top, 5–10 minutes longer. Let rest for 10 minutes before cutting into wedges and serving with extra Chile Jam and warm Cheddar Cornbread Muffins (see page 34).

CHEDDAR CORNBREAD MUFFINS

HANDS-ON TIME: 20 MINUTES

- 2 tablespoons olive oil, plus more for the pan
- 6 ounces sharp Cheddar cheese
- 2½ cups fine cornmeal
- 1 cup all-purpose flour, sifted
- 1 teaspoon baking powder
- ½ teaspoon baking soda
- ½ teaspoon salt
- 2 free-range eggs
- 1 cup buttermilk
- ¾ cup milk
- 2 mild, red chiles, deseeded and chopped
- 2 tablespoons chopped cilantro

Tender little bundles to break open and eat while warm and melty. Scrumptious with Frittata (see page 33) and Easy Tomato, Bell Pepper, and Chile Jam (see page 32).

Preheat the oven to 375°F. Oil a nonstick 12-cup muffin pan. Shred two-thirds of the Cheddar and cut the remainder into 12 cubes.

Combine all the dry ingredients in a mixing bowl and add the eggs, buttermilk, milk, oil, shredded cheese, chiles, and cilantro. Divide among the muffin cups and push a cheese cube into the center of each. Bake until risen and smelling delicious, about 20 minutes. Remove from the oven and let cool slightly on a wire rack. These are best eaten warm.

SUGARED BRIOCHE PERDU WITH CRUSHED STRAWBERRIES

HANDS-ON TIME: 15 MINUTES

FOR THE BRIOCHE PERDU

¼ cup (½ stick) unsalted butter, melted, plus more for the dish
12 slices brioche (about 14 ounces)
5 free-range eggs, lightly beaten
1¾ cups milk
1¼ cups crème fraîche
2 teaspoons vanilla extract
Generous grating of nutmeg
1 cup Demerara sugar

FOR THE STRAWBERRIES

2 pounds strawberries, hulled, halved if large
½ cup sugar
3 tablespoons balsamic vinegar

Sliced brioche, "lost" (perdu) in soothing custard under a sweetly crunchy top, is a little gem, especially served with luscious strawberries, gently crushed and brightened the Italian way with a sprinkle of balsamic vinegar. The day before, make the brioche concoction up to the point of cooking, then refrigerate overnight. Just let the dish sit at room temperature for 20 minutes before cooking.

Generously butter a large gratin or other baking dish. Lay the slices of brioche, overlapping, in the dish. Make sure there are some corners poking up to crisp in the oven.

Whisk the eggs, milk, crème fraîche, vanilla, nutmeg, and ¾ cup of the Demerara sugar together. Slowly pour over the brioche, giving the liquid in the bowl the occasional stir to distribute the sugar evenly as you pour. Cover and refrigerate overnight.

Preheat the oven to 350°F. Take the brioche perdu out of the refrigerator and leave it on the side while the oven heats up. Then sprinkle with the remaining Demerara sugar, drizzle the melted butter over the top, and bake until proudly puffed and golden, about 40 minutes.

Meanwhile, tip the strawberries into a bowl, add the sugar and vinegar, and crush gently with a fork. Let macerate at room temperature while the brioche perdu is baking.

Let the cooked brioche settle for 5 minutes before serving generous squares with the crushed strawberries.

QUICK BREAKFAST IDEAS

Could anyone refuse freshly made **PANCAKES**? To make enough for two very hungry people or three not-quite-so-hungry ones, mix ⅔ cup self-rising flour, 2 tablespoons sugar, and a pinch of salt in a bowl. Make a well in the middle. Break in a free-range egg and slowly pour in ½ cup milk as you stir from the inside out with a fork. When all is smooth and the consistency of heavy cream, heat a heavy, flat griddle or large frying pan over medium heat. Butter it very lightly and drop on spoonfuls of batter to make several pancakes. When the bubbles that rise to the surface of the pancakes begin to burst, flip over (the cooked surface should be golden) and cook for 1 minute longer. Keep the pancakes on a warm plate, covered with a dish towel, while you cook the rest. Serve, in stacks of joy, with butter and syrup or (my favorite) strawberry jam.

Setting up a **BLOODY MARY** station is a clever way to side-step making them. Fill a couple of large bowls with ice cubes; sit a large pitcher of chilled tomato juice in one and a bottle of chilled vodka in the other. Bottles of Worcestershire and Tabasco sauces, cracked black pepper, celery salt, lots of lemon and lime wedges, and an army of tumblers, each containing a celery stick for stirring, will complete the line-up and be enough for most variations. Have extra ice on hand.

Good bread, warmed through or toasted, eaten with warm, **BAKED RICOTTA**, sliced avocado, and the slices of the ripest tomatoes, makes a stunning brunch dish. To bake the ricotta for four, mix 1 cup of the fresh cheese with a free-range egg, a minced red chile (mild or hot), and some minced soft herbs, such as cilantro, parsley, or basil. Season well and spoon into a small, oiled baking dish. Bake at 350°F for about 25 minutes.

You can bend the rules with brunch, moving things up a notch from typical breakfast fare. To make a luscious, sweet and salty **STICKY RICE WITH MANGO** for six, steam 1½ cups glutinous rice in a steamer lined with cheesecloth for about 30 minutes. Combine 2¼ cups canned coconut milk in a saucepan with ⅓ cup sugar and 1¼ teaspoons salt, and stir over gentle heat until the sugar has dissolved. Stir the warm sticky rice into the coconut mixture and serve spoonfuls with slices of ripe mango. To finish, pour a little coconut cream over the top.

Authentic **PORRIDGE** is a world away from instant oatmeal. As the daughter of a Scotsman, I was brought up to prefer my frugal porridge made with water and salt, having first soaked the oats overnight, but admittedly that won't

◇◇◇

be to everybody's taste. If you'd rather be more indulgent, use old-fashioned Scottish oats or rolled oats, add the tiniest pinch of salt, and simmer slowly and gently in milk, or milk and water, stirring often, until done to your liking. Serve with fresh berries—or whatever fruit is in season—and cream, plus perhaps some jam or light brown sugar on the side.

Although taller and more elegant, **POPOVERS** have much in common with the Yorkshire pudding, with both being made from a simple batter. Plain or sweetened vanilla popovers make neat little carriers for fruit preserves and unsalted butter, but I prefer my popovers savory. Preheat the oven to 400°F, and butter and flour a 6-cup muffin pan, the type for giant muffins. Mix ¾ cup all-purpose flour, ½ teaspoon salt, and 3 tablespoons finely grated Parmesan. Whisk together a small handful of shredded basil, 2 extra-large free-range eggs, and 1 cup milk, and add to the dry ingredients, mixing until smooth. Divide among the muffin cups and dust more grated Parmesan over the top. Bake for 10 minutes, then reduce the heat to 350°F and continue baking until the popovers are golden and proudly puffed, 15–20 minutes longer. Make a slit in the side of each popover to let the steam escape and serve warm. They can be reheated as needed and freeze well, too.

Wash a couple of large handfuls of spinach and briefly wilt over medium heat, just with the water that clings to the leaves. Squeeze out any excess water with your hands, then combine the spinach with a generous handful of shredded Monterey Jack cheese, a chopped tomato, 2 beaten free-range eggs, and a few sliced scallions. Season well. Place a frying pan over medium heat, drizzle with olive oil, and put in a soft flour tortilla. Spread with half the spinach mixture and top with a second tortilla, pressing down firmly with a spatula or with your hand. Reduce the heat and cook for a few minutes, then flip over and cook for a couple of minutes longer. Repeat with the remaining filling and more tortillas to make another **QUESADILLA**. Slice them into wedges and serve warm.

The night before, freeze 2 bananas in their skins. In the morning, remove and discard the skins, and chop the bananas into a blender. Add 2 chopped, very ripe figs, 1 tablespoon of honey, the scraped-out seeds from a vanilla bean, ¼ cup chilled milk, and 1 cup plain yogurt. Blend until the mixture is very smooth, adding more chilled milk if it's a bit thick for your taste. Serve the **FROZEN BANANA SMOOTHIE** as soon as possible, in tall glasses.

★

PICNICS AND HAPPY CAMPING

VACATIONS AND WEEKENDS ARE SUPPOSED TO BE JUST THAT. DON'T MAKE THINGS TOO DIFFICULT FOR YOURSELF WITH OVER-AMBITIOUS COOKING WHEN THERE'S A GREAT OUTDOORS TO EXPLORE. RECIPES TO COOK OUTSIDE OR IN MAKESHIFT KITCHENS HAVE TO BE STRIPPED DOWN AND SIMPLIFIED AS MUCH AS THEY'LL ALLOW. MAKE CAKES AND THE LIKE IN ADVANCE AND TAKE THEM WITH YOU, STEERING AWAY FROM ANYTHING WITH DELICATE FROSTING THAT COULD BE SPOILED OR CRUSHED. PACKAGES OF SALT, PEPPER, OIL (IF YOU'LL BE COOKING), AND THE BARE MINIMUM OF PANTRY INGREDIENTS ARE ALL YOU'LL NEED. TAKE A COOLER AND ICE OR FROZEN GEL PACKS IF YOU'RE A SERIOUS CAMPER. HOPEFULLY, THERE'LL BE A FEW FORAGING OPPORTUNITIES—FISH AND MUSHROOMS AND THE LIKE—ALONG THE WAY.

NOW, A LITTLE GENTLE NAGGING. OPEN-AIR FIRES CAN BE DANGEROUS, SO MAKE SURE YOU ONLY BUILD A FIRE OR LIGHT A BARBECUE WHERE FIRES ARE PERMITTED. LEAVE EVERYTHING AS YOU FOUND IT: MAKE SURE THE EMBERS ARE DEAD, RE-COVER THE AREA WITH DIRT OR SAND, AND REMOVE EVERY SCRAP OF TRASH. YOU SHOULD BE ABLE TO TURN AROUND AND WONDER WHERE THE FIRE WAS. ALTERNATIVELY, YOU COULD RENT, BORROW, OR BUY A CAMPER OR RV, THE ULTIMATE IN MOBILE KITCHENS.

EARLY AUTUMN HIKE WITH A PICNIC LUNCH FOR FOUR

Honey, Seed, and Oat Bars

Rosemary Farinata, Mozzarella, Pine Nuts, and Ratatouille Pickle

Iced Peach Tea

As menu titles go, this one's rather dictatorial! But it is the perfect moveable feast to carry in your backpack, and take out to enjoy when you stop for a breather.

HONEY, SEED, AND OAT BARS

HANDS-ON TIME: 15 MINUTES

- ½ cup liquid honey
- ½ cup packed brown sugar
- ½ heaping cup crunchy peanut butter
- ½ cup sunflower oil
- 1 cup Scottish (steel-cut) oats
- 2 cups rolled oats or oatmeal
- ¼ cup wheat germ
- 2 cups mixed seeds (sesame, flax seed, sunflower, pumpkin)
- ⅔ cup dried black cherries

Crisp on top, chewy beneath, the oat mixture will cool to the perfect consistency. If you keep the basic proportions the same, the seeds and dried cherries can be replaced by your choice of nuts and/or other dried fruits. Wrap the bars in foil or paper, individually or in small numbers, to transport. Makes 16–20 bars.

Line an 8-inch square baking pan with parchment paper. Preheat the oven to 325°F.

Warm the honey, sugar, peanut butter, and oil together in a small pan, stirring until blended. Combine all the remaining ingredients in a mixing bowl, pour the honey mixture over, and stir well with a wooden spoon.

Press into the pan and bake until just turning golden, 20–25 minutes. The mixture will set on cooling. Mark into 16 or 20 bars, but let cool completely in the pan before slicing. They will keep for a few days in an airtight container.

To make a refreshing **ICED PEACH TEA**, halve and pit 2 very ripe, fragrant peaches and chop roughly, until the flesh has broken right down. Add ¼ cup sugar to 3½ cups water in a saucepan and bring to a boil. Once bubbling, remove from the heat and stir in 2–3 Darjeeling tea bags, depending on how strong you like your tea, along with the chopped peaches and their juice. Cover with a lid and let steep for 3 minutes. Strain through a fine sieve and cool, then add the juice of ½ lemon. Refrigerate to chill well. Pour into a thermos for drinking later, or serve in four tall glasses, over ice, with fresh mint sprigs and a wedge of peach in each.

ROSEMARY FARINATA, MOZZARELLA, PINE NUTS, AND RATATOUILLE PICKLE

HANDS-ON TIME: 15 MINUTES

2½ cups chickpea flour (besan or gram flour)
1 teaspoon salt
5 tablespoons extra-virgin olive oil
2 tablespoons minced rosemary leaves
Olive oil, for cooking
5 ounces buffalo mozzarella, drained and sliced
Small handful of toasted pine nuts
Ratatouille Pickles (see page 148), well drained, or grilled or roasted Mediterranean vegetables

Should you find yourself making farinata (chickpea flour pancakes) to eat at home, cook them for a bit longer, until really crisp at the edges. Then cut into pieces and serve immediately, with the cheese and vegetables alongside and a drizzle of extra-virgin olive oil over the top. Farinata taste excellent hot or cold, crisp or a little softer.

Put the chickpea flour in a mixing bowl. Combine the salt, extra-virgin oil, and 1⅓ cups warm water in a large bowl. Gradually pour the liquid into the flour, stirring constantly to prevent lumps from forming. The batter should be no thicker than light cream. Pour the batter into the large bowl and stir in the rosemary. Set aside to rest for at least 30 minutes. (You can make the batter a day ahead and keep it cool until needed; stir well before using.)

Heat a little oil in a nonstick frying pan and add a ladleful of stirred batter. Tilt and swirl the pan to create a thin circle, as if you were making a crepe. Cook over medium heat for 4 minutes on each side, flipping over with a spatula, then transfer to a plate. Repeat to make eight golden farinata. Stack them with sheets of parchment paper between them and wrap the stack in foil.

Wrap the cheese, pine nuts, and pickles or vegetables, and pack separately. To eat, wrap or fold the cheese, nuts, and pickles in the farinata.

FLORIS

CAMPER (OR CAMPING) IN THE WOODS FOR FOUR

Oat Cakes with
Ham and Gruyère

Woodland Hash, with a Fried
Egg on Top

Stickiest Gingerbread

If you go down to the woods today... take a frying pan, a wooden spoon, some gingerbread, oat-cake batter, cheese, ham, eggs, salt, pepper, garlic oil, and potatoes with you.

OAT CAKES WITH HAM AND GRUYÈRE

HANDS-ON TIME: 30 MINUTES

1 teaspoon active dry yeast
½ teaspoon sugar
1 heaping cup fine oatmeal (or rolled oats ground to a fine meal in a food processor)
⅔ cup whole wheat flour
½ cup all-purpose flour
½ teaspoon salt
1¼ cups warm milk
Butter, for frying
8 thick slices cooked ham
2 cups shredded Gruyère cheese

These oat cakes are large and soft, rather like crepes. They are delicious rolled up with cheese and ham, as well as baked beans, fried eggs, salad, even jam (not all together, though). Making the batter at home a day ahead would be a good idea; you can put it in a large, screwcap jar and take it with you. Makes 8 oat cakes.

Dissolve the yeast and sugar in ¾ cup warm water. Set aside for 5 minutes.

Combine the oatmeal, flours, and salt in a mixing bowl. Add the yeast mixture. Gradually stir in the milk and about 1 cup warm water to form a batter with the consistency of heavy cream. Set aside for at least 30 minutes, or cover and chill overnight. Stir well before using.

Place a medium frying pan over the heat and rub with a pat of butter. When the pan is hot, pour in a small ladleful of batter and quickly swirl around the pan to form a thin crepe. Cook until golden underneath, about 1 minute, then flip over and cook for 1 minute longer. Transfer to a plate. Repeat to make about eight oat cakes, piling them up in a stack as you go.

Reduce the heat to low and return an oat cake to the pan. Lay a slice of ham on top and scatter a small handful of cheese over it. Heat through gently—the cheese should start to melt—then roll up and eat right away. Repeat until all the oat cakes have been filled and eaten.

WOODLAND HASH, WITH A FRIED EGG ON TOP

HANDS-ON TIME: 10 MINUTES

Garlic and Herb Oil (see below), or olive oil
2½ cups diced unpeeled potatoes
2 large handfuls of mushrooms (ideally porcini, or other mixed mushrooms), sliced if large
4 free-range eggs
Salt and pepper

Using Garlic and Herb Oil makes this a really easy hash, but if you haven't made any, and you use plain olive oil, I recommend adding a crushed garlic clove and a few thyme leaves to the pan with the mushrooms.

Add enough oil to a large frying pan to cover the bottom and set over a medium-high flame. Add the potatoes and stir to coat, then cover with a lid or a layer of foil. Reduce the heat (or raise the pan up from the flames a bit) and cook gently until tender, 15–20 minutes, stirring the potatoes now and then. When the potatoes offer no resistance to the point of a knife, uncover the pan, increase the heat, and sauté until the potatoes are golden all over. Tip onto a plate.

Pour a little more oil into the pan, if necessary, and add the mushrooms. Let cook, pretty much undisturbed, until golden, 3–4 minutes. Push them to the side of the pan and crack in the eggs. Cook until the yolks are done to your liking, then transfer the eggs to plates and return the potatoes to the pan. Quickly heat through with the mushrooms and season. Spoon them onto the plates, beside the eggs, and enjoy.

Pour 1 cup good olive oil into a small saucepan and add 5 peeled and halved garlic cloves and 2 thyme sprigs. Set over very gentle heat and warm through for about 15 minutes. The garlic and herbs should not begin to sizzle at any point. Set aside to cool, then strain the **GARLIC AND HERB OIL** into a sterilized jar or bottle (see page 89). Keep, covered tightly, in the refrigerator until needed and use within 2 weeks.

STICKIEST GINGERBREAD

HANDS-ON TIME: 15 MINUTES

½ cup (1 stick) unsalted butter, cubed
⅓ cup packed dark brown sugar, preferably Muscovado sugar
¾ cup mixed molasses and golden syrup
2 cups self-rising flour
2 teaspoons ground ginger
½ teaspoon ground cinnamon
½ teaspoon baking soda
½ teaspoon salt
2 free-range eggs
½ cup buttermilk
½ cup chopped preserved ginger in syrup, drained and chopped, plus 3 tablespoons syrup
2 teaspoons finely grated fresh ginger

Why use only one type of ginger when you could have three? This is a dark and luscious gingerbread, baked in a square, not a loaf (it's stickier that way). Keep it, wrapped in foil in an airtight container, for up to a week and it will get even better as the days go by. It is perfect for taking with you when camping or hiking.

Line an 8-inch square cake pan with parchment paper. Preheat the oven to 325°F. Melt the butter, sugar, and mixed molasses and golden syrup together in a saucepan over low heat. Let cool slightly.

Sift the flour, spices, baking soda, and salt into a bowl. Add the melted butter and syrup mixture, the eggs, buttermilk, preserved ginger, ginger syrup, and fresh ginger. Mix all together thoroughly and pour into the lined pan. Bake until the cake is risen and springy, about 50 minutes.

Cool in the pan. The gingerbread is delicious eaten fresh (if you can't wait), but for a stronger, really rich flavor, wrap up tightly and keep for 1–3 days before eating.

SPRINGTIME PICNIC AT THE BEACH FOR FOUR

Fire-Charred Mackerel with Radicchio and Pomegranate

Roasted Carrot Hummus

Quick Damper Bread Dipping Sticks

To cook this lunch menu on the beach you'll need a fire or a barbecue, with a grid or a frying pan. Get the freshest mackerel you can, or even better catch them yourself. Damper bread was the staple of stockmen (the Australian equivalent of cowboys), being simple and easy to bake in the embers of a campfire. It's still fun to make.

FIRE-CHARRED MACKEREL WITH RADICCHIO AND POMEGRANATE

HANDS-ON TIME: 10 MINUTES

8 small mackerel, cleaned and gutted
Olive oil
Salt and pepper
3 heads radicchio, trimmed and roughly shredded
Small handful of flat-leaf parsley leaves (optional)
2 tablespoons pomegranate molasses
3 tablespoons extra-virgin olive oil
Lemon wedges for serving

Using sharp-sweet pomegranate molasses in a dressing is a real boon when you're trying to cut down on ingredients: it has such a rich taste that it needs little embellishment. Buy it or make your own by simmering pomegranate juice with a touch of sugar until thick and syrupy. Use four large mackerel instead of eight small ones, if necessary.

Make a couple of diagonal cuts on both sides of each fish. Brush with olive oil and season. Place on a grid (or in a frying pan) and grill over a hot fire or coals for 2–3 minutes on each side. The skin of the fish should be crisp and a little charred. Divide among four plates and place a handful of radicchio and a few parsley leaves (if you have them) alongside the fish.

Combine the pomegranate molasses and extra-virgin olive oil with a little seasoning and drizzle over the fish and radicchio. Add lemon wedges for squeezing over.

ROASTED CARROT HUMMUS

HANDS-ON TIME: 20 MINUTES

- 2 large carrots, scrubbed and thickly sliced
- 1½ teaspoons cumin seeds
- Olive oil
- Salt and pepper
- 1 fat garlic clove, roughly chopped and crushed
- 1 14-ounce can chickpeas, drained
- 1 heaping tablespoon light tahini
- Extra-virgin olive oil
- Lemon juice, to taste
- Quick Damper Bread Dipping Sticks (see right), for serving

Make this in advance to take with you. If you have time, this is even better if you use dried chickpeas, and soak and cook them from scratch.

Preheat the oven to 400°F. Toss the carrots with the cumin seeds and some oil and seasoning. Spread out in a roasting pan and roast until soft and charring at the edges, about 35 minutes. Let cool.

Combine the garlic, chickpeas, tahini, and cumin-spiced carrots in a food processor and pulse until coarse-fine. Add a slug of extra-virgin olive oil and a squeeze of lemon juice, then taste and adjust the balance until you're happy.

Serve with Quick Damper Bread Dipping Sticks, or warmed flatbreads.

QUICK DAMPER BREAD DIPPING STICKS

- 2 cups white or whole wheat self-rising flour
- ½ teaspoon salt
- 1 tablespoon unsalted butter, softened, or vegetable oil (optional)
- ½ cup milk
- ¼ cup water

These are a lot of fun to make. You will need about eight long, firm, clean sticks and a campfire with hot embers.

Measure the flour into a large bowl. Sprinkle with the salt and rub in the butter or oil with your fingertips (or leave out the fat). Put this mixture in a plastic container, ready to take with you.

When ready to cook, add the milk and water, stirring as you do so, to form a dough. Don't overmix. Mold a small handful of the soft dough tightly around the end of each stick. Hold near to the hot embers of the fire and bake, turning carefully, until the bread is golden all over, about 10 minutes. Carefully slide the hot bread from the stick and break open, to eat with the hummus (see left).

You can also make a loaf: double the recipe and shape the dough into a round loaf. Cut a deep cross in the top, wrap loosely in foil, and scrunch together well to seal. Bake in the dying embers of the fire for about 20 minutes; the loaf should sound hollow when tapped on the base. (Or, if more convenient, shape and then bake on an oiled baking sheet at 400°F for 25 minutes.)

VACATION LUNCH FOR SIX TO EAT OUTDOORS

Lamb, Zucchini, and Halloumi Burgers
or Vegetarian Burgers

■

Special Tomato Salad

■

Grilled Corn and Sweet Potato with Fresh Lime Dressing

■

Raspberry Custard Cake

This is easy, bright food for sunny days. Despite being written with a vacation lunch in mind—a cottage on the beach with a barbecue, to be exact—all these recipes could easily be made in a camper kitchen or grilled at home.

LAMB, ZUCCHINI, AND HALLOUMI BURGERS

HANDS-ON TIME: 20 MINUTES

1 zucchini, trimmed and coarsely grated
1½ pounds ground lamb
4 ounces halloumi cheese, coarsely grated (about 1 cup)
Small bunch of mint, leaves shredded
Salt and pepper
⅓ cup Greek yogurt
Squeeze of lemon juice
6 ciabatta or sourdough rolls or burger buns, halved, or pita bread pockets
Young salad greens

Just lamb—use coarsely ground and not too lean for the juiciest burgers—with a few other Greek-ish accents. And good rolls or buns. Simple.

Pile the zucchini into a clean dish towel and squeeze thoroughly to remove the excess liquid. Shake into a mixing bowl and add the lamb, halloumi, and half the mint. Season generously with pepper and not so generously with salt (halloumi is on the salty side), then mix together lightly. Don't overwork the mixture or you'll make the burgers heavy. Shape into six patties. Cover and chill overnight, if you want to get a head start.

Stir the rest of the mint into the yogurt along with the lemon juice, and season to taste.

Grill or broil the burgers for about 4 minutes on the first side and 3 minutes on the second. Toast the cut sides of the bread rolls or buns at the same time.

Put a burger into each roll or bun with a spoonful of mint yogurt and a few salad leaves.

To make four similar **VEGETARIAN BURGERS**, grate a zucchini and squeeze out the liquid, as above. Blitz a thoroughly drained 14-ounce can chickpeas in a mini food processor until coarse-fine, or crush thoroughly with a potato masher. Combine in a mixing bowl with the zucchini, ½ cup shredded halloumi cheese, 1 heaping teaspoon harissa paste, the shredded leaves of ½ small bunch of mint, 1 beaten free-range egg, plenty of pepper, a little salt, and about 3 tablespoons fresh bread crumbs, or just enough to bind. Mix well and form into four patties. Cook in a little olive oil in a nonstick frying pan for 4 minutes on each side.

Crisp, juicy, perfumed, sharp, sweet, and of practically any color you care to name, the types of tomatoes available are wonderfully varied, to say the least. It really is worth seeking out something with more personality than a nameless supermarket fruit. You can make a stunning **SPECIAL TOMATO SALAD** using a few of the different varieties, setting them off with a Calabrian-style oregano dressing (thank you to Francesco Mazzei for the idea). Slice the tomatoes thickly and arrange on a serving plate. Make a simple dressing of red wine vinegar, a smooth extra-virgin olive oil, fresh or dried oregano, salt, pepper, and a touch of crushed garlic, if you wish. Spoon this over the tomatoes and serve.

GRILLED CORN AND SWEET POTATO WITH FRESH LIME DRESSING

HANDS-ON TIME: 20 MINUTES

2 large ears corn, in husks
3 small sweet potatoes, peeled and sliced ½ inch thick
5 tablespoons good olive oil
Salt and pepper
Finely grated zest and juice of 2 limes
1 teaspoon brown sugar
1 long, red chile, deseeded and minced
A few basil leaves, shredded

Don't be shy with the salt in the dressing, because the vegetables need it to balance their sweetness. Grilling the corn and sweet potatoes gives them a delicious, smoky depth of flavor.

Peel the corn husks back and remove the silk inside, then replace the leaves. Dunk the whole ears in water, shake off the excess, and arrange on the grid over hot coals. Grill, turning every now and then, until beginning to blacken all over. Remove from the grill and, when cooled slightly, brush the remains of the husks away. Cut the kernels from the cob with a sharp knife and reserve in a serving bowl.

Toss the sweet potato slices with 1 tablespoon of the oil and season well. Grill for 2–3 minutes on each side, turning with tongs. They will be a little bit crunchy but that's fine. Add to the corn kernels.

Combine the lime zest and juice, sugar, chile, and remaining oil and season to taste. Pour this over the cooked vegetables, scatter some basil on top, and serve.

RASPBERRY CUSTARD CAKE

HANDS-ON TIME: 20 MINUTES

FOR THE CUSTARD

- 2 cups light cream or half-and-half
- 1 vanilla bean, split open lengthwise
- 2 free-range egg yolks
- 2 teaspoons cornstarch
- 2 tablespoons sugar

This unusual recipe makes 10 fabulous slices of cake. As the cake bakes, the custard breaks through the sponge layer and caramelizes at the edge of the pan, while the raspberries form pockets of sauce. Though not the most refined creation, it is marvelous as a simple vacation dessert because it needs no frosting, filling, or adornment. Having said that, more fresh raspberries alongside wouldn't go amiss. For an exotic touch, try flavoring the custard with a tiny amount of rose or orange-blossom water or saffron, then showering the cake with emerald-green pistachios.

Start with the custard. Measure the cream into a small saucepan and place over low heat. Using the tip of a sharp knife, scrape the seeds from the vanilla bean into the cream, then drop in the empty pod. Let heat up gently. Meanwhile, mix the egg yolks, cornstarch, and sugar together in a heatproof mixing bowl.

When the cream is almost—but not quite—boiling, remove from the heat and pour onto the egg mixture, stirring all the while. Pour back into the pan and cook over medium heat, stirring constantly with a wooden spoon, until the mixture bubbles and thickens. Keep boiling for at least 1 minute; the cornstarch will prevent it from curdling. Remove from the heat, cover the surface with plastic wrap or a circle of parchment paper so a skin cannot form, and let cool. Once cool, fish out the vanilla pod.

Preheat the oven to 325°F. Butter a 9-inch springform cake pan and line the bottom with a round of parchment paper. Crush the raspberries roughly with a fork to release their juice. Stir half the crushed raspberries into the cooled custard and set aside.

Beat the butter and granulated sugar together until light and fluffy. Add the eggs, one at a time, beating thoroughly between each addition; stir in a spoonful of flour if the mixture starts to look a bit curdled. Sift in the remaining flour with the baking powder. Pour in the milk and gently mix together to make a batter. Fold in the remaining crushed raspberries until just combined.

Pour half the batter into the pan and make a shallow well in the center with the back of a spoon. Pour the raspberry custard into the well, then cover with the rest of the cake batter. Sprinkle with the Demerara sugar. Bake until golden but still a bit wobbly in the center, about 1 hour.

Let the cake cool in the pan, then chill in the refrigerator overnight, or for at least 4 hours. Remove from the pan when completely cold (you may need to run a knife around the edge to loosen). Cut into slices to serve.

FOR THE CAKE

3 cups raspberries
1 cup (2 sticks) unsalted butter, softened, plus more for the pan
1¼ cups granulated sugar
4 free-range eggs
1⅔ cups all-purpose flour
2 teaspoons baking powder
½ cup milk
¼ cup Demerara sugar

BLACKBERRY–GRANOLA MUFFINS

MAKES 12 PLUMP MUFFINS
HANDS-ON TIME: 20 MINUTES

- 7 tablespoons unsalted butter, melted, plus more for the pan
- Scant 1 cup all-purpose flour
- 1 cup whole wheat flour
- 2 teaspoons baking powder
- Pinch of salt
- ¾ cup packed light brown sugar
- 8 ounces fromage blanc or plain yogurt (about 1 cup)
- 1½ teaspoons vanilla extract
- 2 extra-large free-range eggs
- 1¼ cups granola cereal
- 1 cup blackberries
- 3 tablespoons chopped hazelnuts

What you need when you're camping is a cake, or cakes, that can withstand a bit of rough and tumble. A late-summer blackberry muffin is a perfect start to the day when you've slept in a tent and can't face building a fire. There's a granola recipe in the book (see page 30), but you can use a purchased cereal instead. Vary the berries according to what's in season; use all white flour if you prefer; or replace the granola with white chocolate.

Lightly butter a 12-cup muffin pan, or line with paper cups. Preheat the oven to 350°F.

Sift the flours, baking powder, and salt into a large mixing bowl and tip in the portion that won't pass through the sifter. Stir in the sugar. Whisk the fromage blanc or yogurt, melted butter, vanilla, and eggs together, and add to the dry ingredients along with the granola and berries. Stir quickly until just combined. Don't over-mix—less beating equals lighter muffins.

Spoon the batter into the muffin cups and sprinkle with the nuts. Bake until golden and risen, 20–25 minutes.

Let cool in the pan for 5 minutes, then transfer to a wire rack. Eat warm or cool. The muffins will keep in an airtight container for up to 3 days.

INDOOR PICNIC FOR A RAINY SUMMER'S DAY FOR SIX

RYO (Roll-Your-Own)
Saigon Salad Rolls

Black Rice and Charred Shrimp Salad

Thai-Style Peanut Sauce

Passion Fruit Slice

The rub with Southeast-Asian food is that, while not usually difficult in execution, it does take rather a lot of ingredients to get that hot, sweet, salty, sour balance going. Rather a lot of ingredients means rather a lot of chopping. But that won't matter too much, because chopping is a therapeutic activity and, once ingredients have been chopped accordingly, you'll be able to throw these recipes together in minutes. The reward for a bit of prep will be vibrant, seductively fragrant dishes that won't weigh you down after eating.

BLACK RICE AND CHARRED SHRIMP SALAD

HANDS-ON TIME: 30 MINUTES

This spirited salad is delicious. Thai black rice has a fantastically toothsome texture and nutty flavor. Red rice or brown basmati would make good substitutes if you can't find the black. Sambal oelek (or sometimes ulek) is a fiery Indonesian chile paste that can become quite addictive as an addition to salad dressings, marinades, and stir-fries. Mint and/or Thai basil can be used if you have any cilantro-haters present, such as my brother Ian, who insists it tastes of soap.

FOR THE RICE

3 fat lemongrass stalks
2 cups Thai black rice or glutinous rice

FOR THE DRESSING

⅔ cup canned coconut milk
3 tablespoons fish sauce
1 tablespoon sugar
1½ teaspoons sambal oelek (or 1 red chile, minced)
Thumb-sized piece of fresh ginger, peeled and finely grated
Juice of 1–2 limes, to taste

FOR THE REST

½ cup whole cashew nuts, toasted
2 ripe avocados, pitted and cubed
Bunch of scallions, finely sliced
Large handful of cilantro leaves, roughly chopped
2 pounds raw, peeled black tiger shrimp
2 tablespoons peanut oil
Salt and pepper

Trim the ends of the lemongrass stalks and remove the tough outer layers to reveal the softer core. Rinse and reserve the outer leaves and finely slice the inner part.

Rinse the rice thoroughly in a strainer held under cold running water. Tip into a large saucepan and cover with enough cold water to reach over the knuckle of your upright thumb when you rest the tip of it on the rice. Add the outer lemongrass leaves and a big pinch of salt. Slowly bring to a boil, then reduce the heat and simmer gently for 30 minutes. Drain off any excess water, discard the lemongrass, and let the rice cool.

To make the dressing, whisk all the ingredients together except the juice of 1 lime. Taste and add more lime juice, if you want. Set aside.

Pound the cashews in a mortar with a pestle until roughly crushed, or finely chop them with a knife.

Mix half the dressing with the cooled rice and spoon into a serving bowl. Fold in the avocados, scallions, and most of the cilantro.

Place a ridged castiron grill pan over high heat to get smoking hot. Toss the shrimp with the finely sliced lemongrass and the oil, and season. Space the shrimp out in the hot pan and cook for 1–2 minutes on each side; they should be pink right through and slightly charred. Don't overcook or they will be tough. Tip onto the salad and partially fold into the rice.

Drizzle the remaining dressing over the salad, sprinkle with the cashews, and finish with the remaining cilantro. Serve at room temperature.

The salad here could be worthy of a celebratory dinner if served warm, with the shrimp piled on top or grilled on skewers. A **THAI-STYLE PEANUT SAUCE** on the side may seem like gilding the lily, but will elevate the rice above picnic fare. Toast 1 cup unsalted, dry-roasted peanuts in a 350°F oven until just turning golden. Let cool, then transfer to a food processor. Add ½ cup water, a fat clove of garlic, a dash of toasted sesame oil, 1 heaping tablespoon brown sugar, a dash of soy sauce, a little chopped chile, a squeeze of lime juice, and a generous splash or two of coconut milk. Blitz to make a rustic sauce. Season to taste with a little salt and thin with more coconut milk, if necessary. The sauce will keep, covered, in the refrigerator for a couple of days, but bring it to room temperature before serving.

RYO (ROLL-YOUR-OWN) SAIGON SALAD ROLLS

HANDS-ON TIME: 20 MINUTES

FOR THE DIPPING SAUCE (NUOC CHAM)

¼ cup fish sauce
Juice of 2 limes
3 tablespoons sugar
1 small garlic clove, minced
1 small, red chile, minced

FOR THE SALAD ROLLS

18–24 rice paper rounds
10 ounces firm, marinated or smoked tofu, sliced (optional)
Large handful of mixed herb leaves: Thai or common basil, mint, and cilantro
1 hothouse cucumber, peeled and cut into small sticks
2 long, red chiles, finely shredded
Thumb-sized piece fresh ginger, peeled and finely shredded
4 ounces fine rice noodles, cooked and refreshed (optional)
Handful of garlic chives, in 4-inch lengths (optional)
Butterhead (Boston or Bibb) lettuce leaves, for wrapping

If I can get help putting lunch together, I'll take it, and these fresh, salady rolls lend themselves perfectly to being part of a make-your-own lunch. All you need do is a bit of chopping and make a dipping sauce, then put all the components out in bowls. The main filling event could be cooked shrimp and/or pork or chicken instead of tofu, or just stick with extra crunchy vegetables such as bell pepper and carrot, if you like. A few fine rice noodles will add more substance to each roll.

Start by making the dipping sauce. Combine all the ingredients in a bowl with ½ cup water. Taste and add more of any of the components, as you wish. The sauce should be salty, sweet, and sour with a kick from the chile. Divide among a few little bowls.

Half-fill three wide, shallow bowls with cool water. Have all the filling components ready on a chopping board and/or set out in bowls.

To make each roll, dip a round of rice paper in the water for a couple of seconds, then remove to a plate and wait for half a minute or so, until it becomes pliable. Pile some tofu (or your chosen protein), herbs, cucumber, a very little chile and ginger, and perhaps a few cooked noodles onto one end. Go easy—you don't want to overstuff.

Fold the sides over, then roll up tightly to form a fat cigar, enveloping a garlic chive as you go, if using. Wrap in a lettuce leaf and dip in the sauce to eat.

PASSION FRUIT SLICE

HANDS-ON TIME: 40 MINUTES

FOR THE BASE

2 cups packed graham cracker crumbs
¼ cup (½ stick) unsalted butter, melted

FOR THE CHEESECAKE

3 cups cream cheese
2 free-range eggs, lightly beaten
2 free-range egg yolks
1 tablespoon cornstarch, sifted
1 heaping cup sugar
1 cup fresh passion fruit juice (the strained pulp from about 12 fruits, depending on size)
Seeds scraped from a vanilla bean, or 1 teaspoon vanilla extract

You could dispense with the topping and just serve the cheesecake with some tropical fruit, or even on its own, but I think it's best with the layer of passion fruit gelatin on top. Look for really ripe, perfumed passion fruit, the more shriveled the better. For a smooth-textured topping, strain out the black seeds from the pulp. I rather like their crunch so leave them in. Start this a day ahead.

Preheat the oven to 325°F. Line an 8 x 12-inch, 2½-inch-deep baking pan or dish with parchment paper.

Mix the graham cracker crumbs with the melted butter, then press the mixture evenly over the bottom of the pan. Bake for 10 minutes, then set aside.

Beat the cream cheese in a large mixing bowl until smooth. Beat in the eggs, egg yolks, and cornstarch, followed by the sugar and, lastly, the passion fruit juice and vanilla. Don't over-mix, because too much air in the mixture will make the cooked cheesecake more likely to crack.

Pour the filling over the crumb base and smooth the top with a spatula. Bake until set around the edges but still wobbly in the center, about 30 minutes; the cheesecake should not have browned on top. Turn off the oven and open the door. Leave the cheesecake inside to cool for 15 minutes (this minimizes the chance of the top cracking, although if you add the passion fruit gelatin you won't see any cracks). Remove from the oven and let cool completely before chilling in the refrigerator for at least 1 hour.

To make the topping, soak the gelatin leaves in cold water for a couple of minutes to soften. Heat ¼ cup of the orange juice with the sugar in a small pan until simmering. Remove from the heat. Squeeze excess water from the soaked gelatin and stir into the hot juice mixture until completely melted. Add the remaining orange juice and the passion fruit pulp or juice. Refrigerate for 20 minutes to thicken slightly.

Pour the topping mixture over the cheesecake and return to the refrigerator. Chill for at least 4 hours, or preferably overnight. Cut into 12 bars to serve. Ripe mango or pineapple slices alongside are lovely.

FOR THE TOPPING

3 gelatin leaves
1 cup freshly squeezed orange juice
2 tablespoons sugar
¼ cup passion fruit pulp or juice
Mango or pineapple, for serving (optional)

◇◇◇◇◇◇◇◇◇◇◇◇◇ QUICK CAMPING IDEAS ◇◇◇◇◇◇◇◇◇◇◇◇◇

POTATOES can be baked in the smoky embers of a campfire. Wrap whole baking potatoes or sweet potatoes—you're better off choosing smaller potatoes that will cook relatively quickly—in foil and bury at the edge of the fire. Check after 20 minutes or so and move the potatoes farther away from the main heat if they look charred. Or move them closer into the fire if they don't appear to be cooking. A medium baking potato will take about 50 minutes and a sweet potato 40. You can also toss chunks of any type of potato with olive oil, seasoning, and perhaps some spices and herbs, and wrap in foil, folding the edges over to seal securely but leaving a little room within the package for steam to circulate and help the cooking process. Bury in the white embers, or place on a grill set over the fire, and cook until tender, about 30 minutes.

GREEN CURRY PASTE is a cinch to whip up in advance using a blender, ready to take on any camping trip. Blend 10 deseeded and chopped green chiles, 4 chopped shallots, 3 chopped lemongrass stalks, 5 chopped fat garlic cloves, a thumb-sized chunk of galangal or fresh ginger, 5 kaffir lime leaves, 1 teaspoon shrimp paste (optional), 1 teaspoon coriander seeds, 1 teaspoon cumin seeds, a large bunch of cilantro with stems, 2 tablespoons peanut oil, and the grated zest and juice of a lime. Spoon into a screwcap jar and keep chilled. Use within 5 days for quick curries: enclose cubes of fish, tofu, or chicken in individual foil packages, leaving one end open. Add a little coconut milk, some salt, and 1 teaspoon of the curry paste, then fold the end over to seal very securely. Either suspend over the fire using sturdy sticks, or bury in the hot embers, and cook for about 15 minutes, depending on the contents.

TRAIL MIX, thrown together from white chocolate chips, dark chocolate chips, crystallized ginger, toasted coconut flakes, whole cashew nuts, whole almonds, and dried dark cherries—in whatever ratios suit you best—can prove extremely useful to keep everyone going on long hikes, or can be munched instead of supper if it rains and the fire won't light.

Prick the top of a **WHOLE BRIE OR CAMEMBERT** and poke in a couple of rosemary or thyme sprigs. Sprinkle with a little white wine, if you have any. Making sure no plastic packaging remains anywhere, but leaving the cheese in its wooden box, wrap in foil and bake in the embers of the fire until completely molten in the center, about 15 minutes. Serve with bread or toast for scooping out the cheese.

◇◇◇

JAMAICAN BACON CHICKEN is great for grilling. Despite the name, there's no bacon here, only a can of beer—I think saying beer can in a Jamaican accent sounds like "bacon," which amuses me. Rub a small chicken inside and out with plenty of salt and pepper, a little olive oil, smoked paprika, ground cumin, and crushed garlic. Now drink half the contents of a can of beer, then sit the bird on top of it. The can should be right up the unfortunate chicken's cavity. Stand your chicken upright on a grid set over the glowing coals, but not flames, of the campfire, using the can and the two chicken legs as a sort of tripod. Tent loosely with foil and cook for 1 hour 20 minutes or so; when done, the juices should run clear if the chicken's thigh is pierced with a skewer.

Make a **BLACKENED FISH RUB** for campfire suppers. In a screwcap jar, mix 2 tablespoons each smoked sweet paprika, dried oregano, and English mustard powder with 2 teaspoons each ground cumin, coarsely ground black pepper, and salt. Add 2 pinches of cayenne and mix well. This makes enough for 12 people. Lightly coat any fish fillets (trout, salmon, mackerel...) in melted butter or oil, dust with a little spice rub, and fry in a nonstick pan until cooked through and blackened in places. Eat with an Avocado Salsa (see page 181) and grilled corn.

Any fresh herbs—cultivated or gathered in the wild—will be delicious in a **FRITTATA**. Fennel, dill, thyme, marjoram, oregano, mint, chives, scallions, chervil, and parsley are all ideal, as are wild edible plants like ramps. Lightly beat 8 free-range eggs with salt and pepper and add two handfuls of chopped herbs plus a little shredded cheese, if you like. Heat some butter in a large frying pan until foaming, then pour in the egg mixture and cook gently until the base is golden, about 8 minutes. Flip the frittata onto a plate and slide back into the pan. Cook for a few minutes longer until just set. Remove from the heat and let rest briefly before slicing into wedges.

In a large frying pan, cook a chopped onion in olive oil until softened. Add a generous shake of ras el hanout (Moroccan spice mix), a crushed garlic clove, a handful of roasted bell pepper strips, and a couple of small Spanish-style smoked chorizo sausages, sliced. Cook until the chorizo has released its richly colored oil, 3–4 minutes. Stir in two handfuls of torn sourdough bread and cook until it is toasted, to make **MIGAS**. Divide among four plates and top each serving with a fried free-range egg. Eat with a dab of harissa, if you want some heat.

★

SEASONAL SUNDAY LUNCH

FIRSTLY, LET'S ESTABLISH SOMETHING: I'M NOT SUGGESTING YOU SPEND EVERY SUNDAY MORNING SLAVING OVER A HOT STOVE, OR EVERY SATURDAY SHOPPING FOR FOOD. I AM, HOWEVER, HUMBLY POINTING OUT THAT A HOME-COOKED WEEKEND LUNCH IS A CHARMING TRADITION WORTH PRESERVING, EVEN IF IT'S ONLY A FEW TIMES A YEAR. SO HERE ARE FOUR INDULGENT SUNDAY LUNCHES, ONE FOR EACH SEASON, WHICH MIGHT INSPIRE YOU TO COOK LUNCH AND ENJOY A LAZY AFTERNOON OVER IT, JUST ONCE IN A WHILE. MUCH CAN BE COOKED OR PREPARED IN ADVANCE. THE BEAUTY OF SUNDAY IS THAT, EVEN IF YOU SPEND A FEW LEISURELY HOURS LUNCHING, THERE'S STILL A WHOLE EVENING FOR JUST PUTTERING AROUND AND GENERALLY GETTING THINGS DONE BEFORE THE WEEK BEGINS.

ALL THE MENUS WILL SERVE 6.

AUTUMN SUNDAY LUNCH FOR SIX

Caramelized Baby Roots, Feta, and Sweet Lemon Dressing

Slow-Roasted Red-Currant and Thyme Lamb Shoulder

Glazed Cabbage

Giant Yorkshire Pudding

Pear and Almond Tarte Tatin

A hearty lunch, and rightly so for the time of year, but a nourishing feast rather than over-indulgent. As menus go, this is as adaptable as they come, so substitute any combination of starchy vegetables you like in the warm salad of roots, and replace the Savoy cabbage with red, or with any other winter greens. A pork shoulder roast will respond as tenderly and well as lamb to slow-roasting with wine and robust herbs. Lastly, consider pineapple or apples instead of pears, in the tart.

CARAMELIZED BABY ROOTS, FETA, AND SWEET LEMON DRESSING

HANDS-ON TIME: 20 MINUTES

1 lemon, finely zested, then halved across its middle
5–6 tablespoons olive oil
Leaves from 3 thyme sprigs
1–2 tablespoons mild honey, such as acacia or orange blossom
Salt and pepper
1½ pounds baby root vegetables, such as parsnips, carrots, and turnips, scrubbed
3 cups peeled and cubed butternut squash
12 shallots, peeled and halved
2 teaspoons cumin seeds
7 ounces feta cheese, cubed (about 2 cups)
½ cup roughly chopped, toasted hazelnuts

Sweet young roots are truly delicious in autumn, and are balanced perfectly with salty feta and sharp lemon. If your vegetables have grown to the teenage or young adult stage, halve, quarter or chunk before cooking. If you want to make this the day before, don't add the feta, dressing, or nuts, and refrigerate the vegetables overnight. Warm through in a large frying pan before finishing the recipe.

Warm a large frying pan or wok over medium-low heat. Sear the cut side of the lemon halves in the pan until the flesh is a shade darker than golden. Let cool slightly before squeezing the juice into a bowl. (Don't wash the pan yet.)

Whisk 3 tablespoons olive oil, the lemon zest, half the thyme, and a little honey, to taste, into the lemon juice. Season with lots of black pepper and very little salt. Set this dressing aside.

Bring a large saucepan of salted water to a boil. Add the root vegetables and squash, and simmer for 4–5 minutes. Drain very thoroughly in a colander.

Add 2–3 tablespoons oil to the frying pan or wok along with the shallots. Brown gently, stirring, for 10 minutes, then increase the heat and add the cumin seeds, the well-drained vegetables, a bit of honey, and the remaining thyme. Continue to cook for 10 minutes, tossing now and then. Tip into a warm serving bowl. Fold the feta through gently, then sprinkle with the nuts. Spoon the dressing over the vegetables. Serve warm or at room temperature.

SLOW-ROASTED RED-CURRANT AND THYME LAMB SHOULDER

HANDS-ON TIME: 10 MINUTES

1 large lamb shoulder roast (about 4½ pounds)
1 tablespoon olive oil
Salt and pepper
10 garlic cloves, unpeeled, crushed with the flat of a knife
1 tablespoon red-currant jelly, plus more for serving
1¾ cups white wine
5 thyme sprigs

Autumn lamb is obviously more mature than spring lamb, and all that extra time spent outdoors produces a flavor worthy of a long and aromatic roast such as this. The red-currant jelly adds a touch of sweetness.

Preheat the oven to 325°F. Rub the lamb with the oil and sprinkle with salt and freshly ground black pepper. Set it in a deep roasting pan (or Dutch oven) and add the remaining ingredients along with 2 cups water. Cover loosely with foil (or the lid), sealing well around the edges. Place in the oven and cook until incredibly tender when prodded with a knife, about 4 hours. Increase the oven temperature to 425°F, remove the foil (or lid), and cook until turning golden, about 20 minutes longer.

Remove the lamb from the oven. (You might want to scoop out a couple of spoons of fat from the pan to cook your Yorkshire pudding. See page 77.) Re-cover the lamb with foil and forget about it for half an hour while you cook the pudding.

Just before serving, carefully transfer the lamb to a carving board or serving platter and tent with the foil. Tilt the roasting pan to spoon off as much fat from the surface of the juices as possible, then warm up the juices over low heat (add a bit of water if needed). Serve with the lamb and extra red-currant jelly.

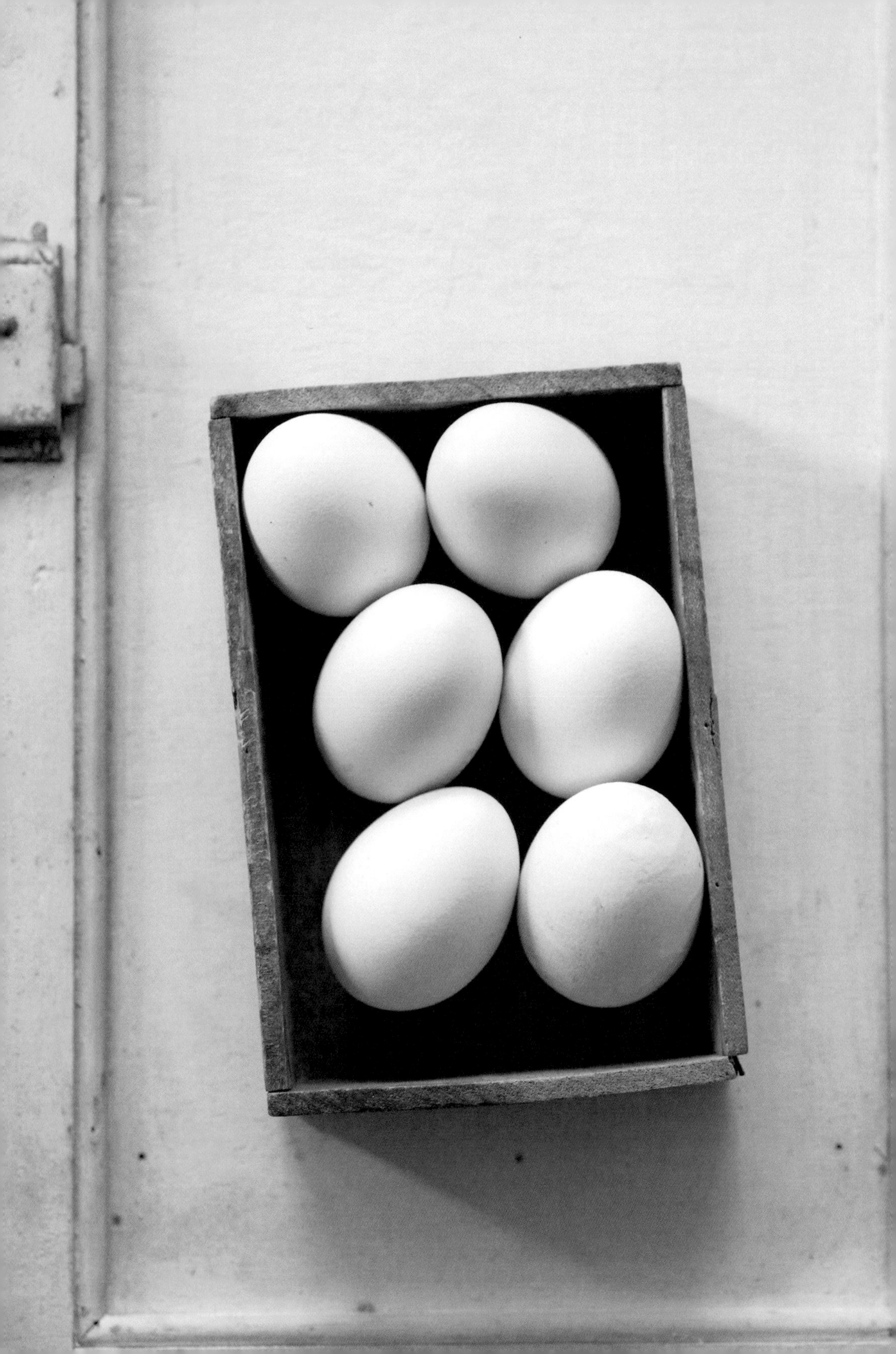

GIANT YORKSHIRE PUDDING

HANDS-ON TIME: 15 MINUTES

1 cup all-purpose flour
Salt and pepper
2 free-range eggs
½ cup milk
2 tablespoons fat from the roast lamb, or peanut oil

This is a man-sized Yorkshire pudding. If you feel like showing off, add chopped herbs, ground spices, grated horseradish, or Parmesan to the batter.

Sift the flour into a bowl and add some salt and pepper. Gently beat in the eggs. Gradually beat in the milk and about ⅓ cup water to form a smooth batter. Alternatively, combine everything (including the water) in a food processor and blend until smooth. Transfer to a pitcher so it will be easy to pour.

I tend to use the batter right away, without resting, but it will sit happily for a few hours. It can even be covered and refrigerated overnight; just leave at room temperature for a while before using.

Heat the oven to 425°F. Pour whatever fat or oil you're using into a roasting pan that is about 11½ x 14 inches and place in the oven to warm up for 5 minutes. Stir the batter well, then quickly pour it into the pan. Put it back into the oven and bake until well risen and golden, 25–30 minutes. Chop the pudding into sections and serve immediately, before it starts to sink.

Serve simply steamed hearty greens, tossed with butter and black pepper. Or make easy **GLAZED CABBAGE.** Simmer a small glass of white wine in a saucepan until reduced by half. Add 1–2 tablespoons butter, a small head of Savoy cabbage, shredded, a grating of nutmeg, and a small, grated pear. Cook gently for 5 minutes, stirring occasionally, then increase the heat and simmer briskly for a few more minutes to evaporate the liquid and form a glaze. Season before serving.

PEAR AND ALMOND TARTE TATIN

HANDS-ON TIME: 40 MINUTES

FOR THE QUICK FLAKY PASTRY

- 1⅓ cups all-purpose flour, plus more for dusting
- Pinch of salt
- ½ cup (1 stick) unsalted butter, frozen

FOR THE PEARS AND CARAMEL

- 6 small, ripe pears
- Lemon juice
- ¾ cup sugar
- ¼ cup (½ stick) unsalted butter
- 10–12 blanched almonds
- vanilla ice cream or crème fraîche, for serving

There's no need to be nervous when making caramel. It's easy, I promise; just keep your nerve—and your fingers away from the hot sugar. You can use refrigerated pie crust, or frozen puff pastry, if you don't want to make your own flaky pastry, although this is a really easy recipe.

Start with the pastry. Sift the flour and salt into a mixing bowl. Coarsely grate the frozen butter into the bowl and use a metal knife to combine it lightly with the flour. Add 1½ tablespoons ice water and continue to mix with the knife until a dough starts to form, adding a few more drops of water as needed. Gently bring it together with your hands, form into a disk, and wrap well in plastic. Refrigerate for at least 20 minutes, or up to 4 days.

Peel the pears and halve from top to bottom. Use a melon baller or teaspoon to remove the cores. Sprinkle with a little lemon juice to stop them browning and set aside.

For cooking the tart, you can use either a shallow, round 8-inch stovetop-to-oven casserole or frying pan with a good, heavy base (this will heat up evenly and prevent any hot spots that could burn your caramel), or a round 8-inch layer cake pan or baking dish. Preheat the oven to 400°F.

If using a stovetop-to-oven pan, sprinkle the sugar over the bottom and set over gentle heat. The sugar will melt slowly; you can help it along by tilting and gently swirling the pan occasionally. Don't stir or the sugar will clump.

When the melted sugar looks like golden brown honey, remove from the heat and quickly stir in the butter. (If using a cake pan or baking dish, make the caramel in a frying pan or saucepan, then pour it immediately into the cake pan or dish and swirl over the bottom.)

Let the caramel cool slightly before packing the pear halves, rounded side down, into the pan. Tuck the almonds into the spaces between the pears.

Roll out the pastry on a lightly floured surface until you can cut out a 9-inch diameter circle. Drape the pastry over the top of the pears, tucking it inside the pan all around the edge. Prick the pastry several times with a fork. (If you are going to bake the tart later, let the pan cool until it is completely cold before covering with the pastry. Then refrigerate for up to 24 hours before cooking.)

Bake until the pastry is golden brown and crisp, about 30 minutes. Let the tart settle for a few minutes before unmolding it upside-down onto a plate with a raised edge (use oven gloves or a dish towel to protect your hands in case the caramel drips).

Serve the tart warm with ice cream or crème fraîche.

IF YOU HAVE TIME TO SPARE A DAY OR TWO BEFORE...

You can cook the root vegetables, make the Yorkshire pudding batter, assemble the tarte tatin so it is ready to bake, and prepare the lamb to the point of being ready to go in the oven—everything will keep in the refrigerator for a night or two. The lamb can even be cooked the day before: just spoon off any solidified fat before covering with foil, then before serving reheat at 350°F for 20 minutes or so.

TIMINGS ON THE DAY

If you want to eat around 2pm...

Start by getting the lamb prepared—aim to have it in the oven by **9AM**. Then you can do something else, like read the Sunday newspapers.

10:30AM If you didn't have a chance to do any advance prep and you're making your own pastry, now is the time to do this and get it chilled.

While that's chilling, make the Yorkshire pudding batter and set aside.

Now (if you haven't made it already), assemble the tarte tatin up to the point when it goes into the oven.

12:30PM The root vegetables can be cooked at this point; you can leave them in their pan to heat through just before serving. In fact, you can do everything except add the cheese, nuts, and dressing; throw these in when you're ready to sit down at the table.

1PM Increase the oven temperature to brown your lamb, then remove it from the oven about 20 minutes later. While the lamb rests, heat up the fat for the Yorkshire pudding, pour in the batter, and put it into the oven. Next get the cabbage started. Transfer the lamb to its serving plate and finish the gravy. Finish the baby root salad on its serving plate and get all hands on deck to take everything to the table. Turn the oven down for the tarte tatin.

When the savory food is winding down, put the tarte tatin in to bake and set a timer for 30 minutes.

HOT PLATES

I'm not the greatest fan of microwaves but they can be useful. Besides melting chocolate and softening the butter I've forgotten to take out of the refrigerator in time, they are good for warming plates. Sit a cup of water on top of a stack of plates and microwave on high for a minute or two.

WINTER SUNDAY LUNCH FOR SIX

Pressed Pork Terrine, Pear Relish, and Bagel Thins

Roast Duck, Prunes, and Chestnuts *or Wild Mushrooms, Prunes, and Chestnuts*

Pumpkin Crescents and Classic Mash

Chocolate and Salted Caramel Cups with Scooping Cookies

Three points of note here, the first being that the menu is seriously rich in parts and seriously delicious in its entirety. The second concerns its distinct unsuitability for vegetarians. The third, regarding the terrine, is to alert you to a bit of advance prep. There are ways around all of these:

1. Eat less later in the day.
2. Replace the terrine with a beautiful, light goat cheese, and the roast duck with earthy mushrooms, for those who would prefer not to eat meat.
3. If you don't have a minute in the four days before the lunch, refer to the first part of point 2.

PRESSED PORK TERRINE, PEAR RELISH, AND BAGEL THINS

HANDS-ON TIME: 30 MINUTES

Too much fat will weigh this terrine down, so look for a meaty piece of pork. It takes an awfully long time to cook, but the results are worth it and the hands-on time is really almost non-existent. If you don't have time to make the Pear Relish, serve with a good store-bought chutney or relish. Thin toast can stand in for toasted bagels.

FOR THE TERRINE
- 1 boned, fresh pork roast (about 3½ pounds)
- 1¼ cups dry white wine
- 2 onions, chopped
- 2 carrots, chopped
- 4 fresh bay leaves
- 20 black peppercorns
- 4 cups chicken stock
- 7 ounces thinly sliced prosciutto
- Handful of parsley leaves, roughly chopped, plus more for serving
- Salt and pepper

FOR SERVING
- 3 bagels, very thinly sliced horizontally
- Spiced Pear Relish (see page 89)

Start with the pork. Preheat the oven to 275°F. Lay the roast in a stovetop-to-oven casserole and add everything but the prosciutto and parsley. Very slowly bring to a boil, skimming to remove any scum. Cover and transfer to the oven to cook for 5 hours or so. When completely tender, transfer the pork to a bowl. Strain the liquid into a wide saucepan, discarding the vegetables and aromatics. Set over medium heat and simmer briskly until reduced by nearly two-thirds, about 20 minutes. Let cool. Remove the skin, fat, and gristle from the cooling pork and discard. Break the meat into large pieces.

Line a 4½ x 9½-inch terrine mold or loaf pan with plastic wrap. Line the bottom and sides with the prosciutto slices, letting excess wrap and prosciutto hang over the top edge. Combine the pork with the reduced cooking liquid and parsley, and season to taste. Pack the mixture tightly into the mold. Fold the excess prosciutto and wrap over the top. Weigh down with cans, or similar, and refrigerate overnight, or for up to 4 days.

Preheat the broiler. Spread the bagel slices on a baking sheet. Broil, not too close to the heat, until beginning to brown, then turn and toast the other sides. (The bagel thins will keep in an airtight container for a week or so.)

Serve the terrine in thick slices with the bagel thins, extra parsley, and pear relish.

CLASSIC MASH

HANDS-ON TIME: 5 MINUTES

- 3½ pounds medium-sized baking potatoes
- About ¾ cup milk, warmed
- 3–4 tablespoons unsalted butter
- Salt and pepper

I prefer the mash a baked potato produces—and you get the bonus of crisp potato skins (drizzle them with oil and salt, and return to the oven to toast)—but if you prefer, cut the potatoes into large, even chunks and simmer in salted water until quite tender; drain very well before peeling and ricing, then whip with milk and butter to create a light mash. I've suggested a smallish amount of butter here, because duck is so rich, but you might want to be a bit more generous when duck isn't on the menu.

Preheat the oven to 375°F. Bake the potatoes until tender, about 1 hour (you can put them in with the duck for its last 30 minutes of cooking, then leave them there while you finish the duck accompaniments). Scoop out the flesh, and rice or mash with the warm milk, butter, and salt and pepper to taste, beating until smooth.

If you can't find a dense, vibrant-fleshed pumpkin, use butternut squash to make roast **PUMPKIN CRESCENTS**. Cut wedges of pumpkin and remove seeds but not skin, then toss with shredded sage, olive oil, balsamic vinegar, and plenty of salt and freshly ground black pepper. Spread the wedges out in a roasting pan and bake at 400°F, turning them over halfway through, until golden and meltingly tender, about 30 minutes.

ROAST DUCK, PRUNES, AND CHESTNUTS

HANDS-ON TIME: 20 MINUTES

1 large duck (about 5 pounds)
Olive oil
Flaked sea salt
1½ cups pitted prunes
1 apple, sliced
2 red onions, finely chopped
Leaves from 2 sage sprigs
7 ounces vacuum-packed cooked, peeled chestnuts
¼ cup armagnac or brandy
4 cups chicken stock

FOR SERVING
Classic Mash (page 83)
Pumpkin Crescents (page 83)
Wilted spinach

Roasting a duck usually means an oven spattered with fat and dry, tough meat. My slow-roast method gently renders the fat away, leaving burnished, crisp skin and tender meat. Cook two ducks if you are having this on its own, without the meaty first course and indulgent dessert.

Preheat the oven to 325°F. Remove the wing tips from the duck. Prick the skin of the fatty parts of the bird to encourage fat to seep out during cooking. Remove any solid fat from the cavity (keep it for roasting potatoes). Put the wing tips in a roasting pan and set a rack on top. Rub the bird with oil and sprinkle with sea salt. Lay, breast-side down, on the rack. Chop three of the prunes and stuff into the cavity along with the apple, half the onions, and the sage leaves. Roast for 2 hours, then pour off the fat and turn the duck over. Roast for 30 minutes longer. Increase the oven temperature to 375°F and continue cooking the duck until golden, about 30 minutes.

Meanwhile, heat a dash of oil in a saucepan and soften the remaining chopped onion for 10 minutes. Throw in the chestnuts and cook for 5 minutes. Add the armagnac and boil to reduce, then add the stock and remaining prunes. Simmer for 10 minutes. Set aside.

Remove the duck from the oven. Pour the contents of the cavity into the saucepan, then let the duck rest on a carving board, tented loosely with foil, for 30 minutes.

Squash the chestnut and prune mixture with the back of a spoon. Pour the fat from the roasting pan and discard the wing tips, then set the pan over the heat. Add the chestnut and prune mixture and simmer, scraping to release the sediment from the bottom of the pan. Chop the duck into pieces and serve with the chestnut and prune gravy.

This makes two helpings of **WILD MUSHROOMS, PRUNES, AND CHESTNUTS**, but can be doubled. I wouldn't reduce the quantities as it gets too complicated to prepare.

Clean 1 pound mushrooms and slice or halve big ones. Include some with character, such as portobello or porcini; wild would be even better. Fry in a little olive oil or butter in your largest frying pan. Keep the heat high and don't stir too often; you want them to color. Tip onto a plate. Reduce the heat and fry a finely chopped red onion in a little more olive oil or butter until soft, about 5 minutes. Add a splash of armagnac or brandy, a minced garlic clove, 3 shredded sage leaves, a few chopped, pitted prunes, and ½ cup chopped, cooked, peeled chestnuts. Stir for a couple of minutes. Season, then stir in 2 teaspoons all-purpose flour. Add 1 cup vegetable stock and simmer for a few minutes to thicken. Return the mushrooms. Sprinkle with chopped, toasted walnuts for a bit of crunch.

To be fancier, boil to reduce the stock to about ¼ cup. Pile the mushroom mixture along the edge of four sheets of phyllo that you have brushed lightly with melted butter or olive oil. Roll up each one like a jelly roll, brush with more oil or butter, set on a baking sheet, and bake at 400°F until golden, about 20 minutes.

CHOCOLATE AND SALTED CARAMEL CUPS WITH SCOOPING COOKIES

HANDS-ON TIME: 40 MINUTES

FOR THE COOKIES

1 cup self-rising flour
¾ cup sugar
½ cup (1 stick) unsalted butter
1 free-range egg yolk
Flaked sea salt

FOR THE CARAMEL

1¼ cups sugar
3 tablespoons golden syrup, or corn syrup
Pinch of flaked sea salt
6 tablespoons unsalted butter
½ teaspoon vanilla extract
½ cup heavy cream

FOR THE MOUSSE

7 ounces bittersweet chocolate
2 tablespoons milk
1 free-range egg yolk
4 free-range egg whites
Tiny pinch of salt
2 tablespoons sugar

A judicious amount of salt is magnificent with both caramel and intense chocolate. Admittedly, this is pretty rich, but it's cold outside (we'll ignore the fact that we probably don't need the bolstering effects of this to keep warm). If you're short of time the day before, just buy some cookies. This recipe makes about 35.

Bake the cookies at least a day ahead to make things easier. Preheat the oven to 375°F. In a food processor, pulse the flour, sugar, and butter to coarse crumbs. Add the egg yolk and blitz to form a dough. Knead briefly, then shape into a sausage, wrap in plastic, and chill in the refrigerator for 30 minutes (or keep in the refrigerator for up to 3 days, or freezer for longer storage). Cut into thin disks and space out on a parchment paper-lined baking sheet. Top each with a little rock of sea salt. Bake until sandy-looking, about 8 minutes. Set aside to cool.

To make the caramel, combine the sugar, syrup, salt, and ¼ cup water in a heavy saucepan over low heat. Once the sugar has dissolved, increase the heat and boil, without stirring, for 5 minutes. The caramel should be a rich amber but no darker. Watch it like a hawk. Remove from the heat and, being very careful, stir in the butter, vanilla, and cream. Divide among cups or glasses and chill.

For the mousse, melt the chocolate in a bowl set over, but not touching the surface of, a pan of simmering water. Add the milk. Remove from the heat and whisk in the egg yolk. Set aside while you beat the egg whites with the salt until soft peaks form. Gradually beat in the sugar. Fold into the chocolate mixture until evenly incorporated. Spoon the mousse over the caramel. Chill for at least 1 hour, or up to 12 hours. Serve with the cookies and little spoons.

IF YOU HAVE TIME TO SPARE A DAY OR TWO BEFORE...

You can make the first course (terrine and relish plus the bagel thins) and the dessert (cookies only or chocolate and caramel cups too). The terrine can be made a full 4 days in advance and kept in the refrigerator.

ROUGH TIMINGS ON THE DAY

Assuming you haven't done any advance prep apart from the terrine and you want to eat around 1pm...

If you start at **10AM**, you can easily have the duck ready to eat by 1:30-ish. Toast the bagel thins for the terrine (or goat cheese), if not done already, and get the duck ready and into the oven around 10:30am.

11AM You'll have made the cookies in advance (or bought some), so now is the time to get on with the rest of dessert. Make the caramel—there's still lots of time because you certainly won't want to eat dessert before 2:30 if you sit down at 1 o'clock. Then make the chocolate mousse and spoon onto the caramel base. Chill.

12PM Increase the oven temperature and put in the potatoes to bake for the mash.

12:15PM Get the pumpkin crescents into the oven. Start preparing the gravy for the duck (finish it while the duck rests). Take the duck out of the oven at 12:30-ish and cover with foil. Finish the gravy.

1PM When the potatoes and pumpkin are cooked, reduce the oven temperature and put plates in to warm. Serve the terrine (or goat cheese), then disappear to the kitchen for a minute to finish the mash and put the pumpkin on a platter.

1:30PM Reheat the gravy and serve the duck onto the warm plates with the mash (make sure you've got at least one helper). Serve the pumpkin at the table.

2:30PM or so, serve the dessert.

A LITTLE NOTE FOR MESSY OR PANICKED COOKS

You're not trying to be a superhero or a Cinderella. This is supposed to be fun. There will be plenty of serving, clearing, and dishwashing to do, so if anyone offers to help, do accept.

If you haven't had time to do much advance prep, there's even more reason to call in the troops, to help with setting the table, chopping onions, mashing the potatoes, and so on.

If you're determined to keep up appearances (and make the rest of us look bad), then at least agree to pile up the dirty saucepans somewhere no one can see them and forget about it all for a bit while you enjoy yourself.

SPICED PEAR RELISH

MAKES ABOUT 3 JARS
HANDS-ON TIME: 40 MINUTES

Pinch of saffron threads
6 large pears, peeled, quartered, and cored
2 cups packed light brown sugar
2 tablespoons coarsely grated, peeled fresh ginger
2 fat garlic cloves, chopped
1 red chile, minced
Finely grated zest of 1 lemon
1 tablespoon coriander seeds, crushed
1¾ cups cider vinegar

You can make this months in advance, or the day before. For the fresher version, reduce the sugar to 1½ cups and the vinegar to ¾ cup. Keep all the other quantities the same but only simmer for 20 minutes. Cool and keep, covered, in the refrigerator for up to a month.

To sterilize clean canning jars and lids, run them through the hot wash in a dishwasher.

Soak the saffron threads in a couple of spoonfuls of boiling water for 2 minutes.

Roughly chop the pears and place them in a saucepan with all the remaining ingredients, including the saffron and its water.

Bring to a boil and bubble away, stirring often, until the liquid has reduced right down and the fruit is soft, about 30 minutes.

Spoon into the hot, sterilized jars and screw the lids on tightly. Process in a boiling-water bath. Let cool, then store in a cool, dark place for up to 6 months. Once opened, keep in the refrigerator and use within a month.

SPRING SUNDAY LUNCH FOR SIX

Sea Bass Baked with
Woody Herbs and Mushrooms

■

Celery-Root Gratin

■

Braised Cavolo Nero

■

Marshmallow Meringues with
Citrus Cream and Rhubarb

Early spring can be gray and wet, with only the occasional sunny day, so this is a menu of seasonal dishes to cheer. Making everything on the day shouldn't be a problem, because there's nothing tricky, although the meringues, citrus cream, and rhubarb can be prepared in advance and put together before serving. The celery-root gratin can be made a day ahead, refrigerated, and reheated when you need it. There's nothing like a couple of dishes in the bag to make everything else easier.

CELERY-ROOT GRATIN

HANDS-ON TIME: 15 MINUTES

1¼ cups vegetable stock
3 large heads celery root (about 2¼ pounds each), peeled and finely sliced
1 tablespoon all-purpose flour
1 cup crème fraîche
3 tablespoons roughly chopped kalamata olives packed in oil
1½ tablespoons minced rosemary leaves
Pepper

This looks like an awful lot of celery root, but I promise it'll be all right. Use a sharp knife to pare the skin from each head as thinly as possible, cutting away the brown and whiskery, rooty bits.

Preheat the oven to 400°F. Bring the stock to a boil in a wide saucepan. Add the celery root, cover, and simmer for 5 minutes. Remove to a bowl using a slotted spoon, and pour the hot stock into a pitcher. Whisk the flour and a pinch of salt into the crème fraîche until smooth, then whisk into the hot stock.

Drizzle a little oil from the jar of olives into a gratin dish. Layer the celery root in the dish, splashing with the crème fraîche mixture, sprinkling with olives and rosemary, and seasoning with freshly ground black pepper as you go. You shouldn't need salt, because the stock and olives are already salty.

Bake until bubbling and golden, 40–45 minutes. Leave in a warm place for at least 15 minutes before serving.

For simply prepared **BRAISED CAVOLO NERO**, a member of the kale family, start with a large bunch (about 1 pound). Trim off the central stems and roughly shred the leaves. Plunge into a pan of boiling salted water and simmer for 6 minutes. Meanwhile, finely slice a couple of garlic cloves and cook gently in a generous dash of olive oil in a large frying pan. Don't let the garlic color too much. Drain the cavolo nero well and add it to the garlic. Toss over medium heat for a few minutes, then season well and serve warm. If this sounds too simple, add canned anchovies and their oil, lemon zest, and dried chile flakes to the garlic in any quantity you fancy. Pancetta or bacon, and perhaps a little crème fraîche, is also good. A similar method works beautifully with cauliflower, broccoli rabe, and other hearty green leaves.

SEA BASS BAKED WITH WOODY HERBS AND MUSHROOMS

HANDS-ON TIME: 20 MINUTES

- 2 fat garlic cloves, finely sliced
- 3 tablespoons olive oil
- 1 pound mixed mushrooms, cleaned and sliced
- 1 cup dry white wine
- Salt and pepper
- 2 sea bass (about 2¼ pounds each), scaled and cleaned
- 4 bay leaves, torn
- Few thyme sprigs
- 2 tablespoons extra-virgin olive oil

Get the freshest fish you can. If no sleek bass are available, try trout or salmon. To get ahead, the mushroom mixture can be fried and the foil package assembled a couple of hours in advance. Keep refrigerated until you are ready to bake the fish.

Preheat the oven to 400°F. Lay two large pieces of foil, overlapping, across a large roasting pan; the foil should be bigger than the pan.

In your largest frying pan, gently fry the garlic in the oil for a minute; do not let it color. Increase the heat and add the mushrooms (you may need to cook them in batches; if crowded they will steam). Fry, stirring now and then, for a few minutes. You want them to color so keep the heat high. When the mushrooms have golden edges add the wine and reduce for a minute to get rid of the alcohol. Pour the mushrooms and their juices onto the center of the foil and season very lightly.

Make three diagonal slashes through the skin on both sides of each fish. Lay the fish on top of the mushrooms. Season each inside and out, then stick a small piece of bay leaf and a few thyme leaves into each slash, tucking the remaining herbs in and around the fish. Drizzle with the extra-virgin oil. Scrunch the foil together to create a loose but tightly sealed package. Bake until the fish are just cooked, 25–30 minutes. To serve, open up the package, and use a knife and slotted spatula to lift sections of fish from the bone. Spoon the mushrooms and their juices onto the plates.

MARSHMALLOW MERINGUES WITH CITRUS CREAM AND RHUBARB

HANDS-ON TIME: 25 MINUTES

FOR THE MERINGUES

4 free-range egg whites
Pinch of salt
6 tablespoons superfine sugar
½ cup confectioners' sugar
½ teaspoon cornstarch
½ teaspoon white wine vinegar
½ teaspoon vanilla extract

The citrus cream here is a touch tart, to counteract the sweet meringue. Any sweet citrus fruit could be used in place of tangerines—satsumas, clementines, or oranges (use half an orange to replace a tangerine). The pink juice of blood oranges would be particularly pretty. You could also serve slices of blood orange instead of the rhubarb.

Start with the meringues. Preheat the oven to 275°F. Line a large baking sheet with parchment paper. Beat the egg whites with the salt and superfine sugar until very dense and holding stiff peaks when you lift out the beaters. Sift the confectioners' sugar and cornstarch on top and continue to beat until the mixture is very stiff and has a shine to it, 3–4 minutes. Beat in the vinegar and vanilla. Spoon into six mounds on the baking sheet, leaving plenty of space around each meringue.

Using the back of a spoon, make a slight hollow in the center of each meringue for the cream and rhubarb to sit in later. Bake until firm, about 1 hour (start checking after 45 minutes). The meringues won't be snow-white any more, but they shouldn't be particularly bronzed. You can make the meringues up to 2 days in advance and store at room temperature in an airtight container.

Now for the rhubarb... In a covered saucepan, gently poach the fruit with the sugar and tangerine juice until just tender, 4–5 minutes. Let cool. If it makes life easier, you can do this ahead of time and then refrigerate the rhubarb for up to 3 days.

Whip the cream, sugar, and citrus juices and zest together until thick. The citrus cream should be floppy in texture rather than firm. Use now, or cover and chill for a few hours, if you need to.

When you're ready to eat, top each meringue with a scoop of the citrus cream and some of the neon-pink rhubarb. Shower each meringue with chopped pistachios and they're ready to go.

FOR THE RHUBARB

1 pound rhubarb (preferably hothouse), trimmed and cut into 1¾-inch lengths
6 tablespoons sugar
Juice of 1 tangerine

FOR THE CITRUS CREAM

1¼ cups heavy cream
2 tablespoons sugar
Juice of ½ lemon
Finely grated zest and juice of 1 tangerine
2 tablespoons chopped unsalted pistachio nuts

SUMMER SUNDAY LUNCH FOR SIX

Stuffed Squash Blossoms; Zucchini and Butternut Agrodolce

Very Garlicky Roast Chicken

Barley Pilaf

Cherry Tart with Jasmine's Almond Pastry

Raspberry Barley Water

If the forecast for the day of your lunch is a scorcher, cook the chicken and pilaf the evening before—or in the early morning—and serve cold. Anyone who has grown their own summer squash will know the moment when enthusiasm for your relentlessly prolific crop turns to apathy. An "agrodolce" (sour-sweet) with vinegar and sugar is the best solution. If you have some vegetarian guests, halve the chicken recipe and add cooked chickpeas, lentils, or lima beans to the pilaf. Because you'll only be able to make a cherry tart when there's a glut, it's a true seasonal joy.

STUFFED SQUASH BLOSSOMS; ZUCCHINI AND BUTTERNUT AGRODOLCE

HANDS-ON TIME: 30 MINUTES

4 zucchini, trimmed and sliced
2¼ pounds butternut squash, peeled, deseeded, and cut in grape-sized cubes
6 tablespoons olive oil
Salt and pepper
2 garlic cloves, sliced
5 tablespoons brown sugar
⅔ cup red wine vinegar
Leaves from a few basil and mint sprigs, shredded
6 ounces mild, soft goat cheese
12 fresh squash blossoms

Delicate squash blossoms are delicious when raw, so I often shred them and fold into salads or pasta. Here I've stuffed and baked them until the edges just sizzle (deep-frying on a sunny day doesn't appeal to me). Do check for any creepy-crawly action before filling. If you can't find any squash blossoms, make a simple salad by combining the agrodolce and crumbled goat cheese with extra basil leaves. On chillier days, this is nice spooned over slices of grilled sourdough bread that have first been rubbed with a halved garlic clove.

Start with the agrodolce because it likes to sit and get to know itself for a bit: a few hours or even a couple of days of contemplation will do it no harm. Preheat the oven to 425°F. Toss the zucchini and butternut with half the oil and spread out in a large roasting pan. Season with salt and pepper. Roast for 10 minutes, then turn the vegetables over and roast for 5 minutes longer. Pull the pan out and sprinkle the garlic, sugar, and vinegar over the vegetables. Mix well. Roast for a final 10 minutes, until sizzling. Stir and let cool, then mix in half the herbs. Refrigerate for up to 2 days, but bring to room temperature before eating.

Combine the cheese and remaining herbs with a little salt and pepper. Remove the stamens from each blossom and carefully stuff with the cheese, unfurling the petals as much as you can to fill the flowers. You'll need the oven at 350°F for the squash blossoms; cook them when you're nearly ready to eat. Arrange them on a parchment paper-lined baking sheet and drizzle with the remaining oil. Bake until just beginning to wilt, about 10 minutes. Serve warm, with the cooled agrodolce spooned over and around.

VERY GARLICKY ROAST CHICKEN

HANDS-ON TIME: 15 MINUTES

2 free-range chickens (about 3 pounds each)
Salt
8 garlic cloves, peeled and crushed, plus 1 whole garlic head, halved horizontally
½ cup (1 stick) unsalted butter, softened
Leaves from 4 tarragon sprigs, chopped
1 lemon, finely zested and halved
Flaked sea salt
1 onion, sliced
1 cup dry white wine
Tossed green salad, for serving

You will have heard it many times, but that's because it's true: it is worth spending extra on free-range birds. The taste will reward you a hundred-fold.

Dry the chickens thoroughly with paper towels and sprinkle with salt. Do this a day or two ahead, if you can, then refrigerate; it will help to crisp the skin. Bring the chickens to room temperature before cooking. Preheat the oven to 400°F.

Mix the crushed garlic with the butter, half the tarragon, the lemon zest, and a generous pinch of sea salt. From the neck end carefully loosen the skin over the breasts and smear two-thirds of the garlic butter under the skin. Put the rest inside the birds along with the lemon and garlic head halves. Spread the sliced onion in a roasting pan large enough to hold both chickens. Set them on top, breasts up, and roast for 20 minutes.

Turn the chickens over and roast for 20 minutes. Turn them the right way up again and roast for 10–15 minutes longer to crisp the skin. Transfer to a plate, draining any juices back into the pan, tent loosely with foil, and let rest for 20 minutes. Spoon the fat from the pan, then mash the onion and soft garlic from the head halves into the juices. Add the wine with ½ cup water. Bring to a boil, scraping the pan, and bubble for a few minutes.

Remove from the heat and stir in the remaining tarragon and any juices from under the chickens. Chop the chickens into pieces and serve with the pan juices, a tossed green salad, and Barley Pilaf (see right).

BARLEY PILAF

HANDS-ON TIME: 15 MINUTES

- ¼ cup (½ stick) unsalted butter
- 1 onion, chopped
- 1¼ cups pearl barley
- 3½ cups chicken or vegetable stock
- 1 cup shelled fresh young peas, or thawed frozen peas
- 2 tablespoons finely chopped mint
- Lemon juice, to taste
- Salt and pepper

I like this simple pilaf with the chicken, but you can embellish it as much as you wish. For example, if you're growing other summery herbs, do add them with the mint. Combinations of citrus zest, spices such as cumin and coriander, grated Parmesan, and toasted nuts or seeds could also be added.

In a large saucepan, melt the butter and cook the onion, stirring often, until softened and tinged with gold, about 8 minutes. Add the barley and stir to coat with the butter. Add the stock and bring to a boil, then reduce the heat and simmer gently until the barley is tender and nearly all the stock has been absorbed, about 40 minutes.

Crush the peas roughly with a potato masher and add to the pan. Continue cooking until no liquid remains, about 5 minutes. Remove from the heat and stir in the mint and lemon juice with salt and pepper to taste. Serve warm or at room temperature.

RASPBERRY BARLEY WATER

HANDS-ON TIME: 20 MINUTES

2½ cups sugar
Strip of pared lemon zest
5 tablespoons pearl barley, rinsed and drained
2 cups raspberries
⅔ cup lemon juice (from about 4 lemons)
Ice cubes, mint sprigs, sliced lemons, and sparkling water, for serving

A fruit-based barley water is very refreshing on a hot day, and can make a great base for cocktails when something a little stronger is called for. This makes about 4 cups.

Place the sugar and lemon zest in a large saucepan with 3 cups water and slowly bring to a boil, stirring now and then until the sugar dissolves.

Simmer briskly for 5 minutes to reduce slightly, then add the pearl barley and remove from the heat. Crush the raspberries lightly, tie them up in a square of cheesecloth, and add to the pan. Let infuse and cool for 1 hour.

Remove the raspberry bag and discard. Add the lemon juice and pour into a sterilized bottle (see page 89). There is no need to strain the barley water. Drink now, or keep in the refrigerator for up to 2 weeks.

To serve, pour a little into tall glasses with ice cubes, mint sprigs, and slices of lemon. Dilute to taste with sparkling water (and add a splash of gin or vodka, if in the mood).

CHERRY TART WITH JASMINE'S ALMOND PASTRY

HANDS-ON TIME: 25 MINUTES

FOR THE PASTRY

1 cup + 3 tablespoons all-purpose flour
¼ teaspoon fine salt
⅔ cup ground almonds
½ cup (1 stick) unsalted butter, diced
6 tablespoons sugar
2 free-range egg yolks
Grated zest of ½ lemon (or ½ teaspoon vanilla extract or kirsch)

FOR THE FILLING

5 cups pitted fresh cherries
1 tablespoon superfine sugar
1 small cinnamon stick, or pinch of ground cinnamon
2 tablespoons red-currant jelly

FOR THE STREUSEL

⅓ cup unsalted butter, melted
⅓ cup sugar
2 tablespoons all-purpose flour
⅔ cup sliced almonds

This tart, from my mum, Jasmine, has the best pastry I've ever tasted: buttery and rich, yet light and lemony. Should you wish to dispense with the streusel topping and second baking, bake the pastry shell completely, for 15 minutes. After simmering the cherries with an extra splash of water, strain off the juice and simmer with 1 tablespoon arrowroot to thicken. Spread the cherries in the tart shell and spoon the thickened juice over them.

Combine all the pastry ingredients in a food processor with 2–3 tablespoons ice water and pulse until just combined. If they don't come together to make a dough, add a tiny bit more water. Don't over-mix or the pastry will be tough. Press into a 9-inch tart pan or dish. (Just break off chunks and spread them out, handling as little as possible.) Trim the edges. Refrigerate for 20 minutes.

Preheat the oven to 375°F and slide in a baking sheet to heat up. Line the pastry shell with parchment paper and fill with dried beans. Place on the hot baking sheet and bake for 8 minutes. Remove the tart shell, leaving the oven on and the baking sheet inside. Lift the parchment and beans out of the pastry shell.

Place the cherries in a pan with the sugar, cover, and cook over low heat until juices begin to run, about 5 minutes. Add the cinnamon and red-currant jelly, and simmer for 2–3 minutes longer. Set aside.

Scrunch a strip of foil around the edge of the tart shell to protect the pastry. Fill with the cherries (fishing out the cinnamon stick, if used). With a wooden spoon, stir the streusel ingredients in a bowl until crumbly. Sprinkle over the cherries and bake until golden, 35–40 minutes.

MELTING CHOCOLATE CAKE

SERVES 8
HANDS-ON TIME: 20 MINUTES

FOR THE CAKE

- ⅔ cup unsalted butter, cubed, plus more for the pan
- 9 ounces bittersweet chocolate, broken into pieces
- ¾ cup sugar
- 5 extra-large free-range eggs, separated
- ⅓ cup ground almonds
- 1 tablespoon bourbon
- Pinch of salt

FOR SERVING

- ⅔ cup heavy cream
- 2 tablespoons confectioners' sugar, sifted
- 1 tablespoon bourbon
- Unsweetened cocoa powder, sifted, for dusting

This rich, oh-so-good cake really is a baked mousse, with only a few ground almonds to take it into cake territory. Great chocolate cakes become old friends and this one has saved me on many an occasion. You can eat it as soon as it has cooled, or refrigerate overnight—the texture will become even more velvety.

Preheat the oven to 325°F. Lightly butter a 9-inch round, springform cake pan. Cut parchment paper to line the bottom and sides. Melt the chocolate and butter in a bowl set over a pan of hot water, or in the microwave. Let cool a little, then stir until smooth. Add 5 tablespoons of the sugar and 1 egg yolk. Gradually mix in the remaining yolks. Stir in the almonds and bourbon.

Beat the egg whites with the salt until they hold soft peaks. Gradually beat in the remaining sugar, 2 tablespoons at a time, beating until stiff and glossy. Loosen the chocolate mixture with a spoonful of egg white, then fold in the rest with a spatula or large metal spoon. Be gentle; you're trying to retain as much of the volume as possible. Pour the batter into the prepared pan and level the top. Bake for 30–35 minutes.

Let the cake cool in the pan, set on a wire rack, for about 15 minutes; it will sink dramatically, but this is exactly what's supposed to happen. Remove the sides of the pan and let the cake cool completely on the pan base. Whip the cream with the sugar and bourbon until just holding a shape and pile into a bowl. Dust the cake with cocoa powder and slice at the table.

◇◇◇◇◇◇◇◇◇ QUICK SUNDAY DESSERT IDEAS ◇◇◇◇◇◇◇◇◇

For those days when you're pressed for time and need a little something sweet...

Don't ever be scared of simplicity. Just make sure your ingredients are the very best. A bowl of perfectly ripe **FRESH FRUIT** of the season, just as it is, or alongside some fantastic ice cream, is more than enough to make a marvelous dessert. Superb quality **CHOCOLATE**, broken into quite large shards and served with good coffee, would be wonderful, too.

If you feel the need to make something more special to eat after your lunch, but don't want too much extra work, the following ideas will fit the bill. Each serves six as written, although they can easily be scaled up or down, depending on the size of the crowd you have to feed.

Roll out a sheet of thawed, frozen butter puff pastry a little thinner than it comes in the package and cut into six even rectangles. Space them out on a large baking sheet. Slice 4 ounces marzipan thinly and divide among the pastry shapes. Slice 6 ripe figs or 8 pitted plums and arrange neatly on top of the **MARZIPAN SLICES.** Drizzle a little honey over the fruit and bake at 375°F until the pastry is puffed and golden and the fruit tender and juicy, 20–25 minutes. Serve warm, with plain yogurt or crème fraîche.

To make **HOT BANANAS WITH CARAMEL-RUM SAUCE**, fry 6 peeled and thickly sliced bananas in a little butter, letting them color undisturbed until golden on each side. This should only take 2–3 minutes. Tip into a bowl and keep warm in a low oven. Return the pan to the heat and add 3 heaping tablespoons brown sugar, a splash of rum, ½ cup light cream, and a large pinch of ground cardamom (leave this out if you don't have any on hand). Bring to a boil, stirring, and simmer for 1–2 minutes, then stir in a small squeeze of lime juice. Divide the bananas among bowls with scoops of vanilla ice cream and spoon the warm sauce over the top. A sprinkle of toasted, chopped pecans would be a tasty finish.

Use a small food processor or blender to make a dense and rich **CHOCOLATE MOUSSE.** Chop 12 ounces bittersweet chocolate into small pieces and scrape them into the processor bowl or blender. Add 3 free-range eggs with a few drops of vanilla extract or 1–2 tablespoons brandy. In a small saucepan, bring 1 cup milk and 3 tablespoons sugar almost to a boil. Pour the hot milk straight onto the chocolate mixture and process for a couple of minutes until smooth. Spoon into little cups and chill for 1 hour. Top with fresh raspberries, if you have any.

◇◇

A truly ripe mango is a wondrous thing, but can be elusive. Canned Alphonso mango pulp (buy it from Indian or other Asian markets or some supermarkets) makes a vibrant substitute in a **MANGO KULFI.** Whip ½ cup heavy cream until billowing and loose. Add a 14-ounce can of mango pulp (or the pulp of about 3 fresh, ripe mangoes) and 1 cup sweetened condensed milk and fold together gently. You could also add a little grated lime zest or ground cardamom. Pour into a plastic container, cover with a lid or plastic wrap, and freeze for at least 6 hours. Serve scoops with ripe, tropical fruit.

Sprinkle a bowlful of Greek yogurt with a layer of dark brown sugar, preferably Muscovado. Add a pinch of ground cinnamon, if you wish, and set aside for an hour. The sugar will melt to form a dark caramel sauce. Swirl through the yogurt with a large spoon—don't overmix—and serve the **CARAMEL YOGURT** alongside banana bread, a fruit crisp, a tart, a compote, or just simple, ripe fruit.

To make **MAPLE SABAYON AND SUMMER BERRIES,** spread summer berries in a large gratin dish or in individual dishes (use a generous handful of berries for each person). Separate 4 free-range eggs, dropping the yolks into a heatproof bowl and saving the whites for meringues (they freeze beautifully in resealable plastic bags). Add ⅔ cup maple syrup and ½ cup white wine to the yolks and set the bowl over a saucepan of simmering water. Beat the mixture until thick and airy, about 7 minutes. Spoon it over the berries and place under a hot broiler until browned in places.

Baked **CHOCOLATE PUDDINGS,** made in six buttered ovenproof cups, can be conjured from a reasonably well-stocked pantry. First preheat the oven to 350°F. Gently heat ½ cup milk and ¼ cup (½ stick) cubed unsalted butter in a small pan, just until the butter has melted. Sift 1 cup self-rising flour into a large bowl and add ½ cup packed light brown sugar and 2 tablespoons unsweetened cocoa powder. Make a well in the center and pour in the buttery milk with a beaten free-range egg, stirring until smooth. Divide among the cups. Combine another ¾ cup packed brown sugar with 2 tablespoons cocoa powder and sprinkle evenly over the puddings. Pour ¼ cup boiling water over each pudding (don't worry—it will look a mess) and bake until domed and just firm on top, about 30 minutes. Dust with confectioners' sugar and serve with cream or ice cream. The cunning cake will have formed its own delectable chocolate sauce underneath.

★

SUPPER AND LUNCH TO SHARE

SUPPER IS FOR SHARING. THERE WILL ALWAYS BE TIMES WHEN DINING ALONE IS A TREAT, AND EVEN A RELIEF—A CHANCE TO EAT CEREAL, ICE CREAM, OR TOAST AT AN INAPPROPRIATE HOUR AND WITHOUT DISAPPROVING LOOKS. FOR THE MOST PART, THOUGH, I BELIEVE IN COOKING AND EATING WITH FRIENDS AND FAMILY, AND AN EVENING MEAL IS OFTEN THE ONLY POINT IN THE DAY WHEN LIFE SLOWS DOWN AND TALK TAKES CENTER STAGE. A SHARED LUNCH IS, SADLY, RATHER A NOVELTY FOR SO MANY OF US THESE DAYS, MOST LIKELY FILED UNDER HOLIDAY CELEBRATION. WHEN YOU DO GET THE CHANCE TO ENJOY A LONGER LUNCH, MAKE THE FOOD SHINE. THERE ARE MANY BEAUTIFUL MENUS AND RECIPES HERE TO TAKE YOU THROUGH THE SEASONS.

BUN NOODLE AUTUMN SUPPER FOR EIGHT

Lemongrass Pork Bun Bowls

Nuoc Cham

The Easiest Frozen Yogurt with a Blackberry Swirl

This is basically a prep list for a relaxed barbecue supper. The idea is to get all the main course components ready and laid out in bowls, for everyone to build their own noodles. Follow with the luscious yogurt ice and berries. You could add some amaretti or shortbread cookies on the side if it feels a bit too light.

LEMONGRASS PORK BUN BOWLS

HANDS-ON TIME: ONE HOUR

FOR THE QUICK PICKLES

½ heaping cup sugar
1 cup rice vinegar
Salt
1 pound carrots, peeled and cut into fine matchsticks
7 ounces daikon (white radish), peeled and cut into fine matchsticks

FOR THE PORK

3½ pounds pork shoulder steaks, trimmed
3 red chiles, minced
4 garlic cloves, minced
4 lemongrass stalks, trimmed to 2-inch bulbous part, finely sliced
1 tablespoon peanut oil
3 tablespoons fish sauce
2 tablespoons sugar
Salt and pepper

FOR THE SCALLION OIL (OPTIONAL)

⅓ cup peanut oil
4 scallions, trimmed and sliced

*"Bun" simply means thin rice noodles, but has come to describe this large bowl of noodles accompanied by dipping sauce, cool salady components, and warm protein of some sort. Admittedly, this requires a bit of chopping and other prep, but nearly everything can be done in advance. You really can't fail with caramelized pork—it's Vietnamese-style heaven, so all the work will be worth it. If you're a woman and any of your guests are men, it's very likely you won't be allowed to barbecue the pork yourself anyway. That is just the law of outdoor cooking. The pickles (*do chua *in Vietnamese), which can be made using all carrot and no daikon, if you prefer, are incredibly addictive. You'll be adding these pickles to everything.*

First, get on with the important business of pickling. Combine the sugar and vinegar with ⅔ cup water and a generous pinch of salt in a bowl, stirring enthusiastically until the sugar dissolves. Add the vegetable matchsticks and set aside for at least 2 hours. (The vegetables can be kept, tightly covered, in the refrigerator for 3 weeks.)

Use a rolling pin to flatten the pork steaks slightly until they're a uniform thickness—about ¾ inch is good. Mix them with the chile, garlic, and lemongrass in a large dish. Let marinate for 30 minutes (or refrigerate overnight).

To make the scallion oil, pour the oil into a saucepan set over medium heat. When hot, add the scallions and cook just until they have wilted, 20–30 seconds. Pour into a bowl and let cool and infuse.

Make the dipping sauce (see page 112). Cook the rice noodles according to the package directions; refresh with cold water and drain. Put all the components—bean sprouts, lettuce leaves, cucumber, pickles, noodles, herbs, peanuts, and dipping sauce—in bowls or on plates on the table like an exotic buffet, ready for everyone to help themselves. Add individual deep serving bowls.

Fire up the barbecue; the coals should be white hot. When you're nearly ready to eat, add the oil, fish sauce, and sugar to the pork and season lightly. Barbecue the steaks for a couple of minutes or so on each side, turning with tongs.

If you're not using a barbecue, heat a large, castiron, ridged grill pan, wok, or frying pan over high heat (turn on the fan over the stove in honor of the fish sauce). Pan-grill or fry half the pork steaks until glazed and caramelized, about 2 minutes on each side. Cover the cooked steaks with foil and keep warm in a low oven while you cook the remaining pork steaks.

Give these assembly instructions: put a small handful of bean sprouts, a few lettuce leaves, and a little cucumber in your own deep bowl. Top with a small handful of cooked noodles (they will feel sticky), a spoonful of scallions and their oil (if using), a spoonful of drained pickles, a few herb leaves, and some pork. Sprinkle with peanuts. Douse with a little dipping sauce and eat.

FOR SERVING

Nuoc Cham dipping sauce (see page 112)
1 pound thin rice noodles (rice sticks)
3 cups bean sprouts
2 large heads of lettuce (butterhead or romaine), washed and leaves separated
1 hothouse cucumber, deseeded and cut into matchsticks
Plenty of mint, cilantro, and shiso leaves (omit the shiso if you can't find it)
1 heaping cup finely chopped, toasted, unsalted peanuts

The compellingly delicious dipping sauce/salad dressing **NUOC CHAM** is based on fish sauce (ideally Vietnamese nuoc mam). Versions abound, but this one makes a good, entry-level sauce to be adjusted to taste. Gently heat ⅓ cup sugar with ½ cup rice vinegar, ⅔ cup water, and ½ cup fish sauce until the sugar dissolves. Do not let the mixture boil. Cool. Add the juice of 1 lime—tasting to see how much you want to add—and stir in 1–2 minced Thai chiles, depending on how hot you want the sauce to be. (When cooking for a crowd, I'd err on the side of mild and offer more minced chiles on the side for the braver souls.) To vary the sauce you can add minced garlic, fresh ginger, and/or finely shredded pickled carrot and daikon.

THE EASIEST FROZEN YOGURT WITH A BLACKBERRY SWIRL

HANDS-ON TIME: 20 MINUTES

FOR THE BLACKBERRIES
1 vanilla bean
2 cups blackberries, plus more for serving
½ heaping cup sugar

FOR THE YOGURT ICE
¾ cup sugar
2 cups plain whole-milk yogurt
1 cup Greek yogurt

This frozen yogurt is utterly fabulous. If you want a richer result, use just the luscious Greek yogurt. I'm sure you already know this, but it bears repeating: save the vanilla bean. Give it a quick rinse and dry well, then push it into a canister of sugar and leave them to get to know each other.

Split the vanilla bean lengthwise and scrape out the seeds with the tip of a knife; set the seeds aside. Put the blackberries in a saucepan and add the vanilla pod and sugar to the pan. Heat gently until the berries start to exude their juices. Crush them slightly with the back of a spoon and let cool. Keep refrigerated until needed.

Beat the vanilla seeds and sugar with the yogurts until evenly mixed. Churn in an ice-cream machine, according to the instructions. If you don't have a machine, pile the mixture into a large freezer container and freeze for about 1 hour. Every half hour after that, whip up the yogurt with a fork, giving it a really good beating to break down any ice crystals and incorporate a bit of air. Repeat this three or four times.

When the blades in the ice-cream machine stop turning, spoon the softly frozen yogurt into a large freezer container. Fish the vanilla pod out of the chilled blackberries, then add them to the yogurt and swirl in gently. Don't over-mix or you'll have uniform purplish yogurt instead of a swirl. Freeze for a couple of hours or overnight. Before serving, if you have left it in the freezer for more than a day, let it soften a bit at room temperature before attempting to spoon it out. Eat with extra blackberries.

LIGHT, POST-CHRISTMAS DINNER FOR FOUR

Cumin-Spiced Baked Fish

Carrot Fritters

Ginger Pachadi

Red Citrus with Brûléed Sabayon

For owners of a mortar and pestle, this is your time to shine in spice-crushing class. A heavy jar base or the side of a wine bottle rolled over a chopping board will do a similar job. If fritter-making feels like too much of a task, steamed brown rice makes a soothing substitute. The carrot batter is well worth the frying time, though, and makes a great canapé base or light lunch when topped with roast chicken, yogurt, and mango chutney.

CUMIN-SPICED BAKED FISH

HANDS-ON TIME: 15 MINUTES

6 sea bass or other whole fish (about 1 pound each), cleaned
1 cup thick, plain yogurt
2 teaspoons cumin seeds, toasted and crushed
1 teaspoon garam masala
2 garlic cloves, crushed
¼ teaspoon hot chile powder
Juice of ½ lime
Salt and pepper

FOR SERVING
Crunchy salad leaves, separated or shredded
Lime wedges
Carrot Fritters (page 116)
Ginger Pachadi (page 116)

This yogurt coating is nicely mild, to allow the fish to shine through, but you can ramp up the spice if that's your thing. Substitute thick salmon or trout steaks, mackerel, or monkfish for the sea bass, if you prefer. But adjust the timing in the oven, because even the thickest steaks or fillets will take less time to cook than whole fish.

Preheat the oven to 425°F. Cut a couple of diagonal slashes on both sides of each fish with a sharp knife. Combine the remaining ingredients and season generously. Rub all over and inside the fish. Space the fish out on an oiled baking sheet and bake until browned and crisp, about 20 minutes. A bit of charring is just perfect: it adds to the flavor.

Plate each whole fish with a small heap of salad leaves, a lime wedge, a few hot Carrot Fritters, and a spoonful of Ginger Pachadi.

CARROT FRITTERS

HANDS-ON TIME: 20 MINUTES

- Peanut oil, for shallow-frying
- 1 pound carrots, shredded (about 5 cups)
- 1 long, red chile, minced (remove seeds, if you like)
- Leaves from ½ small bunch of mint, shredded
- 2 tablespoons sesame seeds
- ¾ cup chickpea flour (besan or gram flour)
- 2 free-range eggs
- ½ teaspoon salt

A long, red chile is likely to be reasonably mild so these fritters won't be fiery, just crunchy at the edges and tender within. Test the chile by trying a tiny bit first, though. Better to scorch your own mouth earlier than everybody else's at supper...

Warm a ¾-inch layer of oil in a high-sided frying pan set over medium heat. Mix all the remaining ingredients together in a bowl with 2 tablespoons water.

Fry heaping tablespoonfuls of the carrot mixture in the hot oil until golden, about 2 minutes on each side, turning with a spatula. You'll need to fry in batches, so move the cooked fritters to a baking sheet and stow in the oven for a couple of minutes while you fry the rest (keep an eye on them because the oven will be set very high for cooking the fish).

A soothing *pachadi* is very similar to a *raita* (both Indian side dishes), counteracting the spices and hot chile it meets on the plate in just the same way. To make a **GINGER PACHADI** for six, mix 1⅓ cups thick, plain yogurt with 2 teaspoons peeled and finely grated fresh ginger, a few shredded mint leaves, the grated zest of 1 lime, and a pinch of salt. Add a small squeeze of lime juice to finish and serve with the fish and fritters.

RED CITRUS WITH BRÛLÉED SABAYON

HANDS-ON TIME: 20 MINUTES

FOR THE FRUITS

2 red grapefruit
3 blood oranges
2 tangerines

FOR THE SABAYON

½ cup sweet wine, such as muscat
⅔ cup packed light brown sugar
3 free-range egg yolks
2 teaspoons orange-blossom water (optional)

Now's the time for really stunning citrus fruit. Choose the best available—about seven fruits will be enough for four people. The brûléeing bit is optional. If you decide to skip it, I suggest that a bit of crunch from some chopped pistachios or walnuts would be a good alternative.

Cut the tops and bottoms from the citrus fruits, then slice away the peel, following the curve of the sides to remove as little flesh as possible. Now cut each fruit into about five wheels, slicing horizontally. Arrange in a large heatproof serving dish, or four individual dishes.

Combine the wine, sugar, and egg yolks in a heatproof bowl set over a saucepan of simmering water. Beat until pale and airy, about 6 minutes. Remove from the heat and beat in the orange-blossom water, if using. Keep beating the sabayon from time to time as it cools a little.

Spoon the sabayon over and around the fruits. Then either use a blowtorch to caramelize the top or place under a hot broiler for a minute or so. Either way, keep a vigilant watch and stop torching or broiling when the sabayon is burnished in places. Take straight to the table.

SIMPLE WINTER DINNER FOR SIX

Stir-Fried Shredded Greens

Chicken and Ginger Clay Pot

Sticky Rice Parcels

Beautiful Pomegranate Gelatin with Cream

The key to a sprightly supper in cold weather is stimulating and warming flavors. Fresh ginger, star anise, chile, and garlic provide the fun for tender chicken and leafy greens here, and everything can be made or prepared in advance. I usually pour the pomegranate gelatin into shallow bowls or cups to set, but don't let that put you off going down the wobbly unmolding avenue... especially when there's this clever trick for unmolding a gelatin dessert: sprinkle water over the serving plate first. Then you'll be able to scoot the gelatin around, to be sure it is in just the right place.

STIR-FRIED SHREDDED GREENS

HANDS-ON TIME: 10 MINUTES

1¾ pounds spinach
2 tablespoons peanut oil
3 garlic cloves, finely sliced
2 red Thai chiles, deseeded and finely sliced
2–3 tablespoons fish sauce
Pepper

All leafy greens love a garlicky stir-fry, so feel free to replace the spinach with other Asian greens, such as bok choy, choy sum, or Chinese kale. If you don't like fish sauce, you can use soy sauce instead. A bit of last-minute wokking will be needed here, but you can get everything ready to go an hour or so beforehand.

Rinse the spinach leaves in a colander, then shred roughly.

Heat the oil and garlic in a large wok or frying pan (adding the garlic to the cold oil should prevent it from burning so easily). Add the chiles when the garlic just begins to sizzle. Cook for half a minute or so, then add the spinach and stir to coat with the oil.

After a couple of minutes, when the leaves have wilted, sprinkle the fish sauce over the spinach. Stand back: it'll be a bit pungent! Season with freshly ground black pepper and serve immediately.

CHICKEN AND GINGER CLAY POT

HANDS-ON TIME: 20 MINUTES

3 tablespoons soft palm sugar or granulated sugar
3 tablespoons light soy sauce
2 tablespoons lime juice
2 tablespoons fish sauce
2 ounces fresh ginger, peeled and finely sliced
4 garlic cloves, sliced
3 star anise flowers
2 Thai red chiles, pierced but left whole
12 skinless, bone-in chicken thighs
1 cup chicken stock
4 shallots or 1 red onion, sliced
Salt and pepper

FOR GARNISH
Thai basil or cilantro leaves
Finely shredded fresh ginger

If you don't have a clay pot, don't worry: a Dutch oven will be fine. This is a fragrant stew with plenty of broth to soak into the Sticky Rice Parcels (see right), balanced between salt, savory caramel, and gentle heat. If you can, marinate the chicken the day before you cook it. Failing that, get it into the marinade as soon as possible—even 20 minutes makes a difference. To make a vegetarian version, use vegetable stock; omit the fish sauce; up the soy sauce to ⅓ cup; and replace the chicken with 1 pound marinated tofu pieces (the kind that have been fried) and 10 ounces shiitake mushrooms. Cook for 30 minutes.

Start the marinade by making a very quick caramel. In a clay pot or Dutch oven (one that fits in the refrigerator), dissolve the sugar in 3 tablespoons water over low heat. Increase the heat and bubble away until the color of honey. Remove from the heat and stir in the soy sauce, lime juice, fish sauce, ginger, garlic, star anise, and chiles. Add the chicken and turn to coat. Marinate at room temperature for 20 minutes, or in the refrigerator for up to 24 hours.

When ready to cook, preheat the oven to 325°F. Add the stock and shallots to the chicken and set on low heat. Slowly bring to a boil. Cover tightly and transfer to the oven. Cook until completely tender, about 1¼ hours. Or simmer very gently on the stovetop for 1 hour, if you prefer. Either way, check after 30 minutes and add a splash of water if it looks dry.

Season with black pepper and, if necessary, a little salt. Garnish each serving with herbs and shredded ginger and serve with Sticky Rice Parcels (see right) and Stir-Fried Shredded Greens (see page 119) to soak up the broth.

Making **STICKY RICE PARCELS** will save you from last-minute rice disasters. Soak 1½ cups glutinous rice in plenty of water for a few hours if you can; overnight is best. The recipe will still work if you can't do this, though. Drain the rice, or just rinse if you couldn't soak it, and tip into a saucepan with 2½ cups stock or water (you can replace 1 cup of this with canned coconut milk, if you like). Add a generous pinch of salt. Bring to a boil and simmer for 8 minutes, then set aside for 10 minutes.

Cut out six pieces of banana leaf or parchment paper. They should each be about 6 x 10½ inches. Spoon one-sixth of the rice onto the end of each leaf and top with a little chopped scallion. Fold to make little packages, tucking in the edges as you go. Either tie each up with string or wrap in a square of foil to secure. Keep in the refrigerator for up to 24 hours, or until you're ready to go, then steam the rice over simmering water for 15 minutes. Snip the string, or remove the foil, and let everyone unwrap their own packages.

BEAUTIFUL POMEGRANATE GELATIN WITH CREAM

HANDS-ON TIME: 15 MINUTES

3 tablespoons sugar
3¼ cups fresh pomegranate juice (squeezed from about 3 large pomegranates)
12 gelatin leaves, or 4 teaspoons unflavored gelatin granules
Juice of ½ lemon
Light or heavy cream, for serving
Pomegranate seeds, for garnish (optional)

You'll need to start this the day before. The recipe makes one large, wobbly gelatin mold, or six person-sized creations. Squeeze the juice from halved pomegranates as if they were lemons, then strain it to remove any stray pith or seeds. But take care: the juice doesn't seem so pretty when it's splattered down your best white T-shirt.

In a saucepan set over low heat, warm the sugar in 1¼ cups of the pomegranate juice until dissolved and steaming, but not boiling.

Soak the gelatin leaves (if using) in cold water until soft, about 3 minutes. Squeeze out excess water, then stir into the hot juice until completely melted. If you are using gelatin granules, sprinkle them evenly over the hot juice and stir to dissolve. Add the remaining cold pomegranate juice, the lemon juice, and 1 cup chilled water.

Pour into a 5-cup mold or six individual molds or bowls. Let cool completely, then refrigerate overnight to set.

Unmold or serve in the bowls. Offer cream to pour over the gelatin and pomegranate seeds to add a crunch.

FIVE SUPPER MENUS FOR TWO TO SHARE

This is a chance to serve a couple of rich, last-minute recipes—those that rely on frying or broiling just before serving. Quite frankly, some could be a nightmare to cook for a large group, but are a pleasure to throw together for two, or even four. Because most of the action revolves around the stovetop, everything can be made straight off, with no advance preparation. There are a couple of more relaxed options for leisurely evenings. I've suggested a first course or a dessert to bolster each main course. I certainly wouldn't worry about producing multiple courses at supper though, so don't feel tied to my ideas.

ROBUST SALAD OF SEARED SQUID WITH SAFFRON DRESSING

HANDS-ON TIME: 30 MINUTES

10 ounces small squid (calamari) with tentacles, cleaned
Small pinch of saffron threads
2 tablespoons olive oil
3 red bell peppers, deseeded and thickly sliced
1 red onion, finely sliced
2 tablespoons red wine vinegar
1 small garlic clove, crushed
Extra-virgin olive oil, to taste
Salt and pepper
2 tablespoons capers, rinsed and drained
Small bunch of arugula, rinsed and drained

Caramelized bell peppers add sweetness and color to this vivacious salad.

Cut the cleaned squid bodies in half lengthwise and score them in a criss-cross pattern. Mix the saffron with 1 tablespoon boiling water in a cup. Set aside to infuse.

Heat 1 tablespoon olive oil in a frying pan and add the bell peppers and onion. Cook over medium-low heat, stirring from time to time, until softened and beginning to brown, 15–20 minutes.

Meanwhile, make the dressing. To the saffron infusion, add half the vinegar and all the garlic with enough extra-virgin olive oil to make a dressing you like. Add a little seasoning and whisk well with a fork.

Tip the onion and peppers into a serving bowl. Return the pan to high heat. Toss the squid with the remaining oil and seasoning, then spread out in the pan. Cook until the squid pieces curl up and char at the edges, 1–2 minutes on each side, turning with tongs.

Return the peppers and onions to the pan along with the remaining vinegar and the capers, and heat through for 1 minute. Tip the mixture into the bowl, add the arugula and saffron dressing, and toss everything together. Serve warm, with crusty bread.

Finish with the ripest **NECTARINES**, halved and pitted, served in bowls topped with **HONEY AND ROSEMARY SYLLABUB**. Whip ½ cup heavy cream until it thickens, then add a squeeze of lemon juice, 2 tablespoons white wine, 1 tablespoon honey, and a pinch of minced rosemary leaves. Whip again until just holding its shape.

SPICED

A little **SHREDDED CABBAGE SALAD** to start or on the side should get you in a Vietnamese mood. Shred ½ small head of white cabbage as finely as you can, discarding the core. Place in a bowl with 1 peeled and finely grated carrot, a handful of chopped mixed mint and cilantro, and 1 tablespoon or so chopped, roasted peanuts. Crush a chopped red chile and ½ garlic clove to a paste with a little salt using a mortar and pestle. Add 1 tablespoon or so fish sauce, a large pinch of sugar, and 3–4 tablespoons rice vinegar. Pour this dressing over the cabbage and toss to combine.

VIETNAMESE CHICKEN AND SWEET POTATO CURRY

HANDS-ON TIME: 20 MINUTES

- 4 skinless, bone-in chicken thighs
- 1½ tablespoons Indian curry powder
- 2 teaspoons soft palm sugar or light brown sugar
- Salt
- 1 tablespoon toasted sesame oil or peanut oil
- 2 shallots, roughly chopped
- 1 fat garlic clove, chopped
- 1 fat lemongrass stalk, trimmed and chopped
- ½ teaspoon dried chile flakes
- 1 large sweet potato, peeled and cubed
- 1–2 tablespoons fish sauce
- 1 14-ounce can coconut milk
- Small handful of cilantro leaves
- Steamed rice, for serving

This is a quick version of a traditional Southeast-Asian chicken curry. Add a little chopped galangal or fresh ginger and/or torn kaffir lime leaves with the garlic, if you have them on hand. You could also substitute large shrimp or cubed pork for the chicken. The curry will have more resonance if you can rub the chicken with the curry powder, sugar, and salt an hour before cooking. It may seem unusual, but Indian curry powder is an authentic addition—it's what they use in Saigon.

Rub the chicken pieces with half the curry powder, the sugar, and a generous pinch of salt. Set aside.

Heat the oil in a wok and add the shallots, garlic, and lemongrass. Stir-fry for a couple of minutes until softened. Add the remaining curry powder, the chile flakes, and the chicken. Stir-fry for a couple of minutes longer.

Now add the sweet potato, 1 tablespoon of the fish sauce, the coconut milk, and ½ cup water. Bring to a boil, then simmer until the chicken is cooked through, 15–20 minutes. Taste and add a little more fish sauce if needed. Scatter the cilantro over the curry before serving with hot steamed rice.

Finish your supper with ripe, fresh fruit.

PAN-FRIED FISH, TAHINI SAUCE, AND RAINBOW CHARD

HANDS-ON TIME: 20 MINUTES

FOR THE TAHINI SAUCE
1 fat garlic clove, crushed with a pinch of salt
2 tablespoons light tahini
Juice of ½ lemon
Salt and pepper

FOR THE FISH
8 ounces rainbow chard or Swiss chard, trimmed
Olive oil, for frying
2 lean white fish, like monkfish or cod, or other small whole fish (about 14 ounces each), filleted
1 tablespoon sesame seeds, toasted
Lemon wedges, for serving

Though I've tweaked it over time, the tahini sauce idea is shamelessly borrowed from Sam and Sam Clark's fabulous Moro: The Cookbook. *Light tahini, that nutty paste of sesame seeds, is an incredibly useful jar of magic to have on stand-by. Give it a good mix before using, because it tends to separate. A spoonful or two works wonders in many kinds of bean purees or dressings. Stir it into yogurt with lemon and parsley to eat with falafel, or use in a garlic-spiked sauce, as here.*

First make the sauce. Combine the garlic, tahini, and lemon juice with 3–4 tablespoons water, enough to give the consistency of light cream. Taste and season.

Rinse the chard. Slice the stems from the leaves and chop into pieces the length of a small thumb. Roughly shred the leaves. Drop the stem pieces into simmering water with a hefty pinch of salt and simmer for 2–3 minutes. Drain and set aside. Add the tahini sauce to the empty saucepan and set over the gentlest heat, just to warm it through.

Warm a little olive oil in a frying pan over medium heat. Season the fish and fry until they are golden brown, about 4 minutes on each side. Place on two warmed plates.

Quickly tip the blanched chard stems into the frying pan along with the leaves and return to the heat. Cook, stirring, for a couple of minutes until the leaves wilt. Add a couple of spoonfuls of the warm tahini sauce and stir well, then divide between the plates. Spoon the rest of the warm sauce over the top. Sprinkle with the toasted sesame seeds and add lemon wedges on the side.

MOORISH

A simple **ARROZ CON LECHE**, essentially a rice pudding, would be just the thing after the light fish dish. Warm 1 cup milk in a saucepan with a cinnamon stick, a few wide curls of lemon or orange zest, and a tiny pinch of salt. When the milk is nearly boiling, stir in 5 tablespoons short-grain rice and simmer, stirring often, until tender and the milk has been absorbed, 15–18 minutes. Add 2–3 tablespoons sugar, according to taste, and stir in a couple of teaspoons of unsalted butter to enrich. Fish out the cinnamon and zest, and grate in a little nutmeg, before serving the rice in warmed bowls, with a fruit compote if you wish.

A VIBRANT SALAD OF DUCK, BLOOD ORANGE, AND OLIVE

HANDS-ON TIME: 25 MINUTES

2 plump duck breast halves
Flaked sea salt and cracked black pepper
2 teaspoons coriander seeds, lightly crushed
2 blood oranges
2 tablespoons extra-virgin olive oil
1 tablespoon sherry vinegar
1 teaspoon honey
1 garlic clove, crushed
2 handfuls of watercress, washed and drained
Small handful of good black olives, pitted
Small handful of sliced almonds, toasted

Years ago, Tom Kime, an inspirational chap and very talented chef, taught me to cook duck breasts this way and I've never wavered since; starting with a cold pan will render much of the fat away to leave you with beautifully crisp-skinned duck. Winter salads can be just as bright and vibrant as their summer cousins, the only difference being that you might want a little extra treat to follow (see right). If a leafy main course doesn't do it for you, fold in some cooked quinoa: toast until golden in a dry pan before simmering in chicken stock.

Preheat the oven to 425°F. Rub the duck breasts all over with sea salt, cracked black pepper, and the crushed coriander. Lay them, skin-side down, in a cold, stovetop-to-oven skillet and set over low heat. As the duck cooks, the fat will render and you'll be able to pour it out into a bowl. (Keep it chilled and covered, for roasting potatoes another time.)

After 10 minutes or so, the skin should be crisp and golden. Turn the breasts and transfer the pan to the oven to roast for 8–10 minutes. After 8 minutes they will be rare, but not too rare. Transfer to a warm plate and let rest.

While the duck rests, cut the tops and bottoms from the oranges and slice off the skin, following the curve of the fruit. Slice the flesh horizontally into wheels and transfer to a bowl. Pour any orange juice on the chopping board into the pan in which you cooked the duck. Add the olive oil, sherry vinegar, honey, and garlic and mix well.

Slice the duck and pour any collected juices into the dressing. Add the watercress to the oranges along with the olives and almonds. Toss with the dressing. Scatter the duck slices over the salad and serve.

LUXURIOUS

A CHOCOLATE PUDDING—or, to be more specific, a pudding of chocolate—is only fitting after that luxurious duck. One idea is to make half the recipe for the chocolate mousse part (forget the caramel) of the Chocolate and Salted Caramel Cups (see page 86) and pile it into two teacups to chill before eating. Best Brownies (see page 182) would be eminently suitable too, especially served warm with ice cream and a simple but rich chocolate sauce. To make the sauce, gently melt 2 ounces bittersweet chocolate pieces in ½ cup light cream along with a generous teaspoon of golden syrup or light corn syrup. Add a dash of rum or brandy and spoon over scoops of vanilla ice cream.

SLOW-COOKED PORK, APPLES, AND CARAWAY

HANDS-ON TIME: 15 MINUTES

- 1 pound boned pork shoulder, trimmed of excess fat
- 1 apple, cut into 8 wedges and cored
- 8 shallots, peeled
- 8 ounces smallish new potatoes, scrubbed
- 2 garlic cloves, roughly chopped
- 1 teaspoon caraway seeds
- Flaked sea salt and pepper
- 2 tablespoons olive oil
- ½ cup dry hard cider
- ½ cup chicken stock

Caraway, pork, and apples make one of those delectable combinations that were just meant to be. There is a long, slow cooking time here, but the entire recipe is very quick to put together. You can use all stock instead of a stock and cider mixture if you prefer.

Preheat the oven to 325°F. Cut the pork into 2-inch cubes and place in a baking dish or roasting pan with the apple, shallots, and potatoes.

Pound the garlic and caraway seeds with a generous pinch of sea salt using a mortar and pestle to form a coarse paste. Stir in the oil. Pour the mixture evenly over the pork, apple, shallots, and potatoes. Add the cider and stock, season with black pepper, and mix well, then spread all out evenly. Cover with foil and bake for 1 hour.

Turn up the oven to 400°F, remove the foil, and give everything a good stir. Continue baking until everything is golden at the edges, 15–20 minutes. Serve with wilted spinach or kale or grated raw beets dressed with lemon juice and olive oil.

RHUBARB SOUFFLÉS are not at all difficult to make. Preheat the oven to 350°F and put a baking sheet inside to warm up. Roughly chop 8 ounces of rhubarb (preferably hothouse) and combine in a saucepan with 5 tablespoons sugar and a splash of water. Cover and heat until just softened. Butter two deep ramekins or ovenproof cups and dust the sides with crushed shortbread or gingersnap cookies. In a clean bowl, beat 2 free-range egg whites with a tiny pinch of salt until they form stiff peaks. Fold in 1 tablespoon sugar, 1 free-range egg yolk, 3 tablespoons vanilla custard sauce or vanilla pudding, and one-third of the rhubarb compote. Drop a spoonful of the remaining compote into each ramekin and top with the egg mixture. Smooth the tops and run your fingertip around the edge to create a groove (this helps the soufflé rise). Set on the hot baking sheet and bake until risen and golden, 16–18 minutes. Serve immediately, with extra custard sauce or pudding poured into the center and the remaining rhubarb compote on the side.

CHILLY SPRING LUNCH FOR FOUR

Easy Dhal Soup

Fish Fry

Curd Rice

Date and Tomato Palm

Sticky Banana Bread with Fresh Mango (and Muscovado Cream for Spreading)

A tricky time of year for cooks. By now, you might be in need of optimistic flavors and colors, but it's still too early to make food warm-weather light. Time to turn East. The spicing of southern India is warm but fresh, often relying on fragrance rather than heat. That's not to say I've been in any way authentic: the dhal soup is a hodgepodge of styles, the fish recipe comes from Chennai, the "palm" or fresh chutney from Orissa, the curd rice from Kerala, and the banana bread from my British kitchen. No apologies though. Together they make a very special and substantial lunch.

EASY DHAL SOUP

HANDS-ON TIME: 15 MINUTES

- 1½ cups yellow split peas, rinsed
- 1 cup canned crushed tomatoes
- ¾ cup canned coconut milk
- 1 onion, finely chopped
- 2 garlic cloves, chopped
- 2 teaspoons cumin seeds, toasted
- ½ teaspoon ground turmeric
- 3 cups vegetable stock
- Lemon juice, to taste
- Salt and pepper
- 2 tablespoons peanut oil
- 2 teaspoons mustard seeds
- 1 red chile, minced (remove the seeds first, if you like)

It might take a while to cook, but there's nothing difficult here. Just put it all together and it'll practically take care of itself. It might help, timewise, to make it a day or two in advance, reheating and tempering the spiced topping just before serving. Leftovers freeze perfectly, too.

Tip the split peas, tomatoes, coconut milk, onion, garlic, cumin, turmeric, and stock into a large saucepan and bring to a boil. Simmer, partly covered with a lid, until the split peas have broken down, about 40 minutes, stirring now and then. Season to taste with lemon juice, salt, and pepper. It shouldn't be necessary, but you can thin with a little water to adjust the consistency. Heat through again and divide among four warmed bowls.

Heat the oil in a frying pan and fry the mustard seeds and chile until the seeds pop and dance. Spoon this over the hot soup and eat.

FISH FRY

HANDS-ON TIME: 15 MINUTES

- 4 skate wings (8–10 ounces each)
- 1 teaspoon ground turmeric
- 2 garlic cloves, crushed
- 1 teaspoon peeled, finely grated fresh ginger
- ½ teaspoon mild chile powder
- ½ teaspoon crushed black pepper
- 2 teaspoons lemon juice
- 1 tablespoon peanut oil
- 2 tablespoons unsalted butter
- Salt
- Leaves from 1 sprig fresh curry leaf

Eating this on the coast of Tamil Nadu in southeast India can't easily be beaten for authenticity. I just wish I'd made a better job of writing notes at the time. It's taken several attempts to turn "Chunks of fish. Skate? Southern spice crust—typical. Charred. Juicy..." into a useful recipe. But I got there in the end and it really is very delicious.

If necessary, trim the skate wings with sharp scissors, enough to tidy them and remove the frill, which tends to burn at the edges and makes the fish too big for most pans.

Mix the turmeric, garlic, ginger, chile powder, black pepper, and lemon juice in a small bowl. Pour this over the fish, rubbing it in well. Set aside for at least 20 minutes, or up to a couple of hours, but not overnight; you want the fish to remain as fresh as possible. Divide the oil and butter between two frying pans. Shake the fish dry and season with salt. Add the curry leaves to the pans, followed by the fish, and fry over medium heat until golden, about 5 minutes on each side. Turn the heat down if the fish gets too dark; you want to cook it through and get a bit of a crust without burning. Serve with the curry leaves, Curd Rice (see page 138), and Date and Tomato Palm (see left).

To make **DATE AND TOMATO PALM**, a quick, fresh chutney that zings with ginger, heat 2 teaspoons oil or butter in a saucepan and fry 2 teaspoons cumin seeds until fragrant. Add 1½ tablespoons peeled and chopped fresh ginger, 3 roughly chopped tomatoes, ⅓ cup chopped, pitted Medjool dates, ¼ teaspoon ground turmeric, 1 tablespoon brown sugar, and a pinch of salt. Cook, stirring, until thick. Let cool before serving. You only need a little chutney to go with the rice and fish so this makes a small amount, but you can increase the quantities and keep the chutney refrigerated for up to 10 days.

CURD RICE

HANDS-ON TIME: 15 MINUTES

- 1 heaping cup basmati rice, rinsed and drained
- ½ teaspoon salt
- 1 tablespoon peanut oil
- 1 green chile, halved lengthwise
- 1 teaspoon mustard seeds
- Leaves from 1 sprig fresh curry leaf
- 1 cup plain yogurt
- Small handful of cilantro, chopped

This is a simple version of curd (yogurt) rice that goes well with the spiced fish and punchy chutney. If you want to get more elaborate for another time, try adding grated fresh coconut, grated carrot, cumin seeds, and cashew nuts in any combination. If the recipe below seems like too much work, just follow the first paragraph to prepare plain basmati rice.

Tip the rice into a saucepan and add the salt and 2½ cups cold water. Bring to a boil, then cover and simmer gently for 10 minutes. Remove the pan from the heat and let it rest undisturbed for 5 minutes.

Meanwhile, heat the oil in a small frying pan, add the chile, mustard seeds, and curry leaves, and cook until the mixture sizzles and pops.

Fluff up the rice with a fork. Fold the yogurt into the rice with the hot spice mix and the cilantro.

STICKY BANANA BREAD WITH FRESH MANGO (AND MUSCOVADO CREAM FOR SPREADING)

HANDS-ON TIME: 20 MINUTES

- 2 free-range eggs
- 7 tablespoons unsalted butter, melted
- 1 cup packed dark brown sugar, preferably Muscovado sugar
- ½ teaspoon salt
- 1 teaspoon vanilla extract
- 4 large, very ripe and soft bananas, mashed
- 2 tablespoons crème fraîche
- 1⅓ cups all-purpose flour
- 1 teaspoon baking powder
- ½ teaspoon ground cinnamon
- 1 heaping cup chopped, toasted macadamia nuts (optional)
- 1 ripe mango, peeled, pitted, and sliced

If you don't want to use nuts, leave them out or replace with 2 tablespoons unsweetened, shredded coconut. Spring is prime time for the most luscious, honeyed mangoes.

Line a 9 x 5 x 3-inch loaf pan with parchment paper. Preheat the oven to 350°F.

Beat the eggs, melted butter, sugar, salt, and vanilla together until light and airy, 3–4 minutes. Beat in the bananas and crème fraîche. Sift the flour, baking powder, and cinnamon over the top and fold in thoroughly. Fold in two-thirds of the nuts, if using.

Pour into the pan and sprinkle with the remaining nuts. Bake until a skewer poked into the center comes out clean, 50–60 minutes. Unmold and cool on a wire rack before slicing. Serve in bowls with slices of ripe mango and Muscovado Cream (see below).

Before you start preparing the cake, make the **MUSCOVADO CREAM**. Stir 2 tablespoons light or dark brown sugar (ideally Muscovado sugar) into 1 cup crème fraîche or Greek yogurt along with the finely grated zest of 1 lime and half of its juice. Cover and keep refrigerated until needed (up to 2 days).

LIGHTEST ELDERFLOWER AND RASPBERRY MERINGUE ROULADE

SERVES 8–10
HANDS-ON TIME: 20 MINUTES

4 extra-large free-range egg whites
Pinch of salt
1¼ cups superfine sugar
2 teaspoons cornstarch
1 teaspoon white wine vinegar
1 teaspoon vanilla extract
Confectioners' sugar, for dusting
1 cup heavy cream or crème fraîche
¼ cup Elderflower Syrup (see page 183)
2 heaping cups fresh raspberries, plus more for serving

Similar to a pavlova, this fluffy, cloud-like meringue cake baked in a jelly roll pan is incredibly quick to make. You could make it a few hours in advance: roll it up with a sheet of parchment paper and keep in a cool place until you're ready to unroll, fill, and roll up again.

Preheat the oven to 350°F. Use parchment paper to line a jelly roll pan that is about 9 x 13 inches. Cut the paper so that it stands about 1¼ inches above the rim of the pan.

Beat the egg whites with the salt in a very clean bowl until stiff peaks form. Gradually beat in the superfine sugar, then continue beating until you have a very thick, shiny meringue, about 2 minutes. Add the cornstarch, vinegar, and vanilla, and beat in briefly. Spread the meringue in the lined pan. Bake until firm to the touch, about 20 minutes. Let cool in the pan.

Place a large sheet of parchment paper on the work surface and dust with confectioners' sugar. Unmold the meringue onto this and carefully peel off the lining paper.

Whip the heavy cream with the elderflower syrup until it just holds its shape; if you're using crème fraîche istead of heavy cream, just beat in the syrup. Spread over the meringue, leaving a clear border at the edges to stop the filling oozing out at the sides of the finished roulade. Top with the raspberries in an even layer. Roll up from one of the long sides, using the paper to help form an even log. Transfer to a plate and scatter some extra raspberries over the roulade. Cut into thick slices to serve.

A LATE SUMMER SUPPER FOR EIGHT

Roasted Tomato Gazpacho with Pesto

Beet-Cured Side of Salmon and Waxy Potatoes

Aioli and Shaved Fennel Salad

White Peach and Very Vanilla Tart

This, both for taste and looks, is one of my favorite menus in the book. The colors and lightness suit a relaxed party perfectly. With luck, the night will be warm enough for you to enjoy your supper outside. You can make pretty much everything up to 3 days in advance: the gazpacho, pesto, cured fish, aioli, and all the components of the tart (crumb crust, poached peaches, and pastry cream). On the day you'll only have to boil potatoes, make a fennel salad, slice the salmon, and put the tart together before serving.

ROASTED TOMATO GAZPACHO

HANDS-ON TIME: 20 MINUTES

4 pounds reddest, ripest, late-summer tomatoes, halved
2 mild red chiles, deseeded and roughly chopped
5 tablespoons extra-virgin olive oil
Salt and pepper
Thick slice of artisan bread (such as ciabatta)
3 red bell peppers, deseeded and roughly chopped
1 red onion, roughly chopped
1 fat garlic clove, crushed
1 large hothouse cucumber, roughly chopped
3 tablespoons sherry vinegar, to taste

FOR SERVING
Basil leaves
Pesto (see right)

Late August and September bring tomato bliss. Choose the most fragrant vine-ripened tomatoes you can find for this soup. Roasting the tomatoes for a gazpacho is not conventional, but it really intensifies their sweetness. It's best to make this at least a day in advance, if you can: a good gazpacho needs a long chilling time.

Preheat the oven to 400°F. Spread the tomatoes, cut sides up, in two roasting pans and tuck the chiles underneath (or they will shrivel and burn). Drizzle with 2 tablespoons olive oil and season well with salt and freshly ground black pepper. Roast for about 30 minutes. The tomatoes will be a little charred, which is how they are supposed to be. Let cool. Meanwhile, soak the bread in ½ cup of cold water.

Combine everything in a food processor or blender and add ½ cup water. Pulse until almost—but not quite—smooth. Taste and season with salt and freshly ground black pepper, plus a dash more vinegar, if you want. Chill for at least 2 hours, but preferably overnight. Up to 3 days in the refrigerator will only do it good.

If the gazpacho is too thick, dilute with a little ice water before serving, chilled, in bowls with basil leaves and a spoonful of Pesto on top.

PESTO

HANDS-ON TIME: 10 MINUTES

2 garlic cloves, peeled
Flaked sea salt and pepper
3 tablespoons pine nuts
Leaves from 2 large bunches of basil (about 3 heaping cups)
6–8 tablespoons extra-virgin olive oil

Because this is intended to be served with gazpacho (see left), it doesn't feature any cheese—that seems to be a flavor too intense in this case. But for other uses you can stir in a couple of tablespoons of freshly grated Parmesan at the end. It will perk up risottos, simple pasta dishes, grilled meats, and much more.

Using a large mortar and pestle, crush the garlic to a puree with a large pinch of sea salt; the salt crystals will help break the garlic down. Gradually add the pine nuts and basil as you continue to pound. The finished texture is up to you—as coarse or smooth as you like. A splash of water will help with the pounding and lightens the pesto a touch. (If you prefer, crush the garlic with the flat of a knife, then pulse with the pine nuts and basil in a food processor.)

Stir in enough oil to loosen the pesto, along with freshly ground black pepper and a little more salt, if needed.

Transfer to a jar and pour a film of olive oil over the surface of the pesto. Cover tightly and keep in the refrigerator for up to 5 days. Stir before using.

BEET-CURED SIDE OF SALMON AND WAXY POTATOES

HANDS-ON TIME: 10 MINUTES

- 1 very fresh side (whole fillet) of salmon (about 2½ pounds)
- 2 tablespoons fennel seeds
- 1 tablespoon black peppercorns
- ¾ cup packed light brown sugar
- 1 cup flaked sea salt
- Small bunch of dill, chopped
- 2 small beets, scrubbed and trimmed
- 4½ pounds small new potatoes

FOR SERVING

- Lemon wedges
- Aioli (see right)
- Shaved Fennel Salad (see right)

The beets stain the cured fish purple-pink, making it look very pretty. The contrast of crisp salad, sweet-salty fish, unctuous aioli, and hot potatoes is wonderful, but if it is just too sultry for hot food, dress the potatoes with olive oil and serve cold.

Check the salmon flesh for bones and use tweezers to remove any that were lurking undiscovered. Lay the fish, skin-side down, in a non-metallic dish. Roughly crush the fennel seeds and peppercorns using a mortar and pestle (or a rolling pin on a cutting board). Mix with the sugar, salt, and half the dill in a bowl.

Grate the beets and add to the sugar mixture. Spread this over the salmon, tucking a little underneath the fish, too. Cover with plastic wrap and weigh down with a baking pan containing a couple of cans of beans or something similar. Refrigerate for at least 24 hours, or up to 3 days.

Brush off the beet mixture. Rinse the fish briefly under cold water and pat dry with paper towels. Sprinkle with the remaining dill. Keep refrigerated until ready to serve.

Cook the potatoes in boiling salted water until tender, 15–20 minutes; drain and serve hot, just as they are. While they are cooking, lay the salmon, skin-side down, on a cutting board and slice very thinly at a 20–30 degree angle to the board, starting at the tail end. Serve on the board or a platter with lemon wedges. Put the Aioli, Shaved Fennel Salad, and potatoes on the table in bowls for everybody to help themselves.

AIOLI is a dreamy and fail-safe stand-by. Crush a small garlic clove (you can always add more later) with flaked sea salt, using the flat of a knife. Whisk a free-range egg yolk in a bowl to break it down. Very slowly whisk in 1¾ cups mild olive oil—drop by drop at first, then, as the mixture starts to thicken, in a thin trickle—until thick and wobbly. You may not need all the oil. Stir in the garlic and add salt, pepper, and a little lemon juice to lift the flavor. I also like to add a small amount of finely grated lemon zest or a little chopped dill.

To make a simple **SHAVED FENNEL SALAD**, trim any coarse outer layers and root from 4 bulbs of fennel, reserving the frondy tops, and halve each bulb from top to bottom. Using a very sharp knife, the slicing blade of a food processor, or a peeler, cut the fennel into very fine slices. Mince the fronds and mix with the shaved fennel. Before eating, dress with a touch of lemon juice, extra-virgin olive oil, salt, and freshly ground black pepper. Toss a handful of baby arugula leaves through to finish.

WHITE PEACH AND VERY VANILLA TART

HANDS-ON TIME: 30 MINUTES

FOR THE CRUMB CRUST
- 8 ounces sweetened oat crackers, finely ground in a food processor, or 3 cups graham cracker crumbs
- 7 tablespoons unsalted butter, melted

FOR THE PEACHES
- 1¼ cups sugar
- 1¼ cups white wine
- 1 vanilla bean, split open lengthwise
- 8 ripe but firm white or yellow peaches

This tart is heavenly. I'd highly recommend making it as it's written, although there are ways to simplify it. For example, you can replace the pastry cream (crème pâtissière) with cream that has been whipped with vanilla seeds and a touch of sugar. If your peaches are very ripe, don't bother to poach them; just pit and slice. By the way, the poached whole peaches are also delectable with vanilla ice cream and shortbread cookies.

For the crust, mix the crumbs with the melted butter. Press firmly over the bottom and up the sides of a deep, 9-inch tart pan with a removable base. Cover and refrigerate for at least 3 hours to firm up (it can be kept for up to 3 days).

To poach the peaches, combine the sugar, wine, vanilla bean, and 1¼ cups water in a large saucepan. Bring to a boil very slowly to dissolve the sugar, then simmer for 10 minutes. Cut a shallow cross in the base of each peach and add to the simmering liquid. Poach gently, turning occasionally, until just tender, about 5 minutes.

Remove the peaches from the pan with a slotted spoon. When they have cooled for a minute, peel them and return the peach skin to the pan (it will turn the syrup a pretty blush color). Increase the heat and boil the syrup to reduce by one-third. Let cool and strain into a bowl. Add the whole peaches and the vanilla seeds scraped from the pod. The peaches can be refrigerated overnight.

To make the pastry cream, heat the milk, salt, and vanilla bean in a saucepan; remove from the heat when the mixture starts steaming just before it boils. Set aside to infuse for 20 minutes or so, if you have the time. In a heatproof bowl, whisk the egg yolks and sugar together until pale and thickened. Whisk in the flour.

Remove the vanilla bean from the milk and scrape the seeds back into the pan with the tip of a knife. Reheat the milk gently. Pour a little into the whisked egg yolks, while whisking, then pour in the rest of the milk. Return to the saucepan. Bring to a boil, stirring, and simmer briskly until thickened, about 2 minutes. Lay a circle of parchment paper or plastic wrap directly over the surface of the pastry cream to prevent a skin from forming and let cool. The pastry cream can be kept in the refrigerator for up to 3 days.

To assemble the tart, fold the crème fraîche into the cooled pastry cream. Carefully remove the crumb crust from the tart pan—you can leave the base in place—and transfer to a plate. Spoon in the pastry cream and spread it out evenly. Halve and pit the peaches and arrange, cut-sides down, over the pastry cream. Spoon some of the peach syrup over the peaches just before serving.

FOR THE PASTRY CREAM

1 cup whole milk
Tiny pinch of salt
1 vanilla bean, split open lengthwise
3 free-range egg yolks
3 tablespoons sugar
2 tablespoons all-purpose flour
⅔ cup crème fraîche

SUPPER AND LUNCH PRESERVE

RATATOUILLE PICKLES

MAKES 4 LARGE JARS
HANDS-ON TIME: 20 MINUTES

- 4 cups wine vinegar (I use half red and half white)
- 3 tablespoons salt
- 1 cup sugar
- 1 tablespoon black peppercorns
- 2 tablespoons coriander seeds
- 2 red onions, cut into sixths
- 4 red, yellow, or green bell peppers, thickly sliced
- 2 firm zucchini, thickly sliced
- 2 small, firm eggplants, halved and cut into thick sticks
- 8 garlic cloves, unpeeled but crushed lightly
- 4 rosemary or thyme sprigs, or 5 bay leaves

This is so-called because it uses sunny ratatouille-like ingredients. It is very little trouble to make, and you'll be glad you did: drizzled with extra-virgin olive oil the pickled vegetables are wonderful eaten with good cheese or cured ham, a peppery salad, olives, and some good bread. If you prefer, you can adjust this recipe to make a more traditional, Italian-style antipasto: reduce the sugar to 1 tablespoon and drain the vegetables after simmering; discard the vinegar mixture and instead submerge the vegetables in their jars in extra-virgin olive oil.

Combine the vinegar, salt, sugar, peppercorns, coriander seeds, and 2 cups water in a large, non-reactive pot and slowly bring to a boil, stirring to dissolve the sugar and salt. Once simmering, add the vegetables, garlic, and herb sprigs or leaves. Continue to simmer for 5 minutes.

Ladle the mixture into sterilized jars (see page 89), seal firmly with lids, and turn the jars upside down to cool.

Keep in a cool, dark place for up to 6 weeks. Once opened, keep refrigerated and use within a month.

QUICK PACKED LUNCH IDEAS

Because the following suggestions are all rather amiable characters, they would be eminently suited to a starring role as supper the night before their matinée appearance in your lunchbox.

Make too many **MEATBALLS** for supper one night, on purpose. Mix coarsely ground steak with minced onion and garlic and a pinch of fresh or dried oregano. Bind with egg and bread crumbs before rolling into balls. Brown in olive oil, then simmer in a tomato and red wine sauce for 20 minutes. The next day, spoon the leftovers into a robust bun or roll—something Italian would be fitting—with fresh basil leaves and grated Parmesan. Wrap well and pack some napkins for tomatoey fingers.

Leaves quickly lose heart once dressed so, unless you take a separate dressing in a little jar, I'd stick to grains and legumes for a **PORTABLE SALAD**. Simmer lentils, quinoa, or pearl barley in stock until tender. Fold into a tangle of sliced onions and bulb fennel that you have gently fried until golden. Add chopped parsley and sun-dried tomatoes, roughly crushed, toasted walnuts, and a peppery-sweet dressing of wholegrain mustard, balsamic vinegar, and olive oil. Thickly sliced Italian sausages or crumbled feta, stirred in at the end, will stand up to all those robust flavors, and the salad is fabulous hot or cold.

Most **SOUPS** like to sit and get to know themselves for a day or two so, if you have a thermos, or the means to reheat a bowlful, consider this hearty Tuscan recipe. Soak 2 heaping cups dried chickpeas overnight. Drain and rinse well, then cover with a thumb's-length of fresh water and bring to a boil. Add a couple of chopped onions, carrots, and celery stalks. Follow with a can of crushed tomatoes, 4 slices of bacon, sliced, and a sprig of rosemary. Cover and simmer until the chickpeas are soft, about 3 hours. Puree in a blender and season to taste. Meanwhile, heat olive oil in a pan and fry slices of ciabatta until golden. Drain on paper towels and rub with the cut sides of a halved garlic clove. Take the bread with you, well-wrapped, and submerge in the hot soup before eating. Drizzle with extra-virgin olive oil, too, if you can.

Another **BOISTEROUS SALAD**. Toast pine nuts until golden and stir into cooked lima beans, red onions sliced whisper-thin, the ripest tomatoes, chopped, and chopped tarragon. Make a dressing of crushed garlic, a very few dried chile flakes, wholegrain mustard, good balsamic vinegar, and extra-virgin olive oil. This is even better tossed with arugula leaves, flaked tuna, Parmesan, or leftover roast lamb or chicken.

QUICK SUPPER IDEAS

Rosemary brightens this simple, but very good **LEMON LINGUINE.** You'll probably have all the ingredients for this sitting in your kitchen. Cook 7 ounces linguine in plenty of boiling salted water, according to the package directions. Finely grate 2 ounces Parmesan into a large, warmed bowl. Add the finely grated zest of ½ lemon, the juice of 1 lemon, 1 teaspoon minced rosemary leaves, and 4 tablespoons extra-virgin olive oil, whisking everything together until combined. Season to taste. Drain the cooked pasta in a colander but don't shake it too thoroughly dry; tip it into the large bowl with a bit of water still clinging to it—this will help the consistency of the sauce. Toss the pasta with the lemon-rosemary mixture and serve.

Buy a whole **CHINESE ROAST DUCK** from a Chinese restaurant, and remove the good bits in large, boneless pieces. Warm them through in a hot oven to crisp up the skin. Meanwhile, combine toasted sesame oil (or use light tahini or peanut butter instead), lime juice, a little crushed garlic and/or fresh ginger, soy sauce, minced chile, and chopped cilantro. Toss this through cooked soba noodles along with cooked, shredded greens (bok choy is good). Add large shreds of the warmed duck and sprinkle with toasted sesame seeds. If you want to eat this as a cold dish, don't bother to warm the duck.

Fresh lasagne sheets can make a **QUICK CRAB CANNELLONI** for two. Gently simmer 2 cans of crushed tomatoes with a dash each of extra-virgin olive oil and white wine, a pinch of saffron threads, and seasoning for 15 minutes. Meanwhile, combine 8 ounces crab meat with ¼ cup mascarpone, a few drained sun-dried tomatoes in oil, 2 tablespoons grated Parmesan, and chopped parsley. Season with black pepper. Cook 6 fresh lasagne sheets in boiling salted water for a couple of minutes; drain, refresh under cold water, and dress with olive oil to stop them sticking. Roll one-sixth of the crab mixture in each sheet and place in an oiled baking dish. Spoon the sauce on top and heat under the broiler until toasted at the edges, about 10 minutes.

An **ASIAN SQUASH SOUP** starts with pan-grilling 2 halved shallots until blackened in places. Peel away the skin and add to a saucepan with some heated peanut oil. Fry gently for 5 minutes, then add 2 diced tomatoes and a peeled, deseeded, and diced butternut squash. Pour in a can of coconut milk; refill the can with stock or water and add, along with a couple of kaffir lime leaves and a handful of cilantro. Simmer gently until tender, about 15 minutes. Remove the lime leaves and blend until smooth, adding a little fish sauce to taste.

PARTY

GREAT FOOD MAKES ANY PARTY. KEEP IT CASUAL: LOTS OF FOOD FOR SHARING, LOTS OF BOOZE AND FRUIT JUICES, AND PLENTY OF ICE FOR MIXING. GONE ARE THE DAYS OF FANCY CANAPÉS AND UPTIGHT ONE-UPMANSHIP. ENTICING, COLORFUL RECIPES THAT GET PEOPLE MAKING, SERVING, AND HELPING WILL CREATE A RELAXED ATMOSPHERE... AND HELP YOU OUT IN THE PROCESS. IT'S YOUR PARTY AND YOU SHOULD ENJOY IT.

THESE ARE SUBSTANTIAL MENUS FOR SPECIAL PARTIES, NOT NECESSARILY TO BE EATEN (OR DRUNK) SITTING AROUND A TABLE.

AUTUMN MOVIE NIGHT FOR EIGHT

Parmesan and Pepper Popcorn

■

Spiced Nuts

■

Salt-Roasted Potatoes with Smashed Herb Crème Fraîche

■

Butternut and Sage Strata with Garlicky Toasts

■

Roasted Onions

■

Caramel-Almond Pears

Cozy, indulgent, sharing food for grazing as you laze in front of the TV. These dishes won't mind sitting about with you. The recipes would also all work beautifully eaten around a fire outdoors. Just add mugs of hot soup and some mulled cider to keep everyone feeling toasty.

PARMESAN AND PEPPER POPCORN

HANDS-ON TIME: 5 MINUTES

1 teaspoon sunflower oil
½ cup popcorn kernels
¼ cup unsalted butter, in small cubes
¾ cup freshly grated Parmesan
1 teaspoon coarsely ground mixed peppercorns
Salt

Real popcorn is essential for movie night. Pick out any unpopped kernels before serving; they're a bit hard on teeth if unwittingly chewed.

Measure the oil into a large saucepan, preferably one that has a handle on either side, and set over high heat. Add the popcorn kernels, cover, and listen for the popping to start.

Once the corn begins to pop, start to shake the pan over the heat and keep shaking constantly until the popping slows down again. Remove from the heat. Scatter the remaining ingredients over the popcorn, adding salt to taste. Put the lid back on the pan and shake to toss everything together thoroughly. Pour the popcorn into a very big bowl and serve.

SPICED NUTS, toasted with a touch of sweetness and herb, are perfect for snacking. Toast 10 ounces (2–2½ cups) mixed nuts—macadamias, almonds, and cashews make a good partnership—in a dry frying pan. Keep the heat low and shake the pan often to be sure the nuts don't burn. When the nuts are fragrant and pale golden-brown, add a drizzle of olive oil, a pinch of chile powder, a shake of dried oregano, and 1 tablespoon honey. Keep toasting gently, shaking and stirring, until the nuts are caramelized all over. Tip onto a baking sheet to cool, and serve in bowls.

SALT-ROASTED POTATOES WITH SMASHED HERB CRÈME FRAÎCHE

HANDS-ON TIME: 15 MINUTES

FOR THE POTATOES

4½ pounds coarse rock salt
Handful of thyme sprigs
3½ pounds small baking potatoes, scrubbed

FOR THE SMASHED HERB CRÈME FRAÎCHE

2 garlic cloves
Handful of soft herbs (mint, chives, basil, parsley, oregano)
Finely grated zest and juice of 1 lemon
Salt and pepper
2 tablespoons extra-virgin olive oil
1¾ cups crème fraîche

Despite what you might expect, these potatoes don't taste overly salty after cooking. After baking in their cloak of herby salt, their skins will be wrinkly and their insides buttery-gorgeous.

Preheat the oven to 400°F. Spread half the salt in a deep roasting pan and scatter the thyme on top. Nestle the potatoes in the herbed salt and cover with the remaining salt. Bake until tender, about 45 minutes (check by prodding a potato with a skewer). The cooking time will obviously depend on the size of your potatoes.

Meanwhile, crush the garlic, herbs, and lemon zest with a pinch of salt using a mortar and pestle. Add the olive oil and work to a rough puree. Stir this into the crème fraîche along with a squeeze of lemon juice and a little black pepper. Cover and set aside until needed.

When the potatoes are done, brush off the salt and pile into a warm bowl. Serve the crème fraîche on the side.

BUTTERNUT AND SAGE STRATA WITH GARLICKY TOASTS

HANDS-ON TIME: 30 MINUTES

- 2 cups milk
- Thick slice of sourdough bread, diced small
- 6 extra-large free-range eggs
- 1 cup ricotta cheese
- Salt and pepper
- 1 small butternut squash
- Olive oil
- 1 large red onion, finely chopped
- 7 ounces slab bacon, cut into small sticks
- Small handful of sage leaves
- 4–5 ounces buffalo mozzarella, torn into pieces
- ½ cup freshly grated pecorino or Parmesan
- Garlicky Toasts (page 160), for serving

If a glance down the ingredients list introduces any doubt about the merits of a hearty, bread-lined bake accompanied by more bread, worry not. A few cubes of sourdough give the cooked custard extra body and, once you have spread a warm spoonful or two onto crisp Garlicky Toasts, all will be understood. This is best made, up to the point of cooking, the day before, which should make matters easier. It's an obvious point, but leaving the bacon out will make this vegetarian-friendly.

Measure the milk into a large bowl and stir in the bread, eggs, and ricotta with a little salt and coarsely ground pepper. Don't mix it thoroughly; a few golden streaks of egg yolk are a good thing. Set aside in a cool place.

Preheat the oven to 400°F. Peel the squash, halve, and scoop out the seeds, then cut into wedges. Toss with olive oil and seasoning, and roast in a foil-lined pan for about 30 minutes. Meanwhile, cook the onion and bacon in a bit of oil in a large frying pan. Keep the heat gentle for 5 minutes until the onion softens, then turn up the heat to get the bacon sizzling. Shred half the sage and add to the pan, then tip into the milk bowl.

Spread half the milk and bread mixture in a large, oiled gratin dish and nestle in half the squash and mozzarella. Repeat, then sprinkle with the pecorino. This can be baked now, but will be better if you refrigerate it for a while, overnight if possible.

Bake the strata at 350°F until golden and bubbling, 40–45 minutes. Meanwhile, sizzle the remaining sage leaves in olive oil for a few seconds; drain on paper towels and scatter on top of the strata. Spread scoops of warm strata onto Garlicky Toasts and eat.

The most tender **ROASTED ONIONS**, naturally sugared at the edges and fragrant with thyme, are both vegetable side dish and sauce. Preheat the oven to 400°F. Peel 8 red onions and cut a deep, vertical cross in each. Cram a small thyme sprig into each cross with a sprinkle of salt and pepper. Sit the onions in a baking dish, drizzle with extra-virgin olive oil and balsamic vinegar, and cover with foil, sealing it well. Bake until soft and caramelized, 50–60 minutes. Eat the onions as they are or scooped onto Garlicky Toasts (below) with Butternut and Sage Strata (see page 158).

To seek enlightenment through the medium of **GARLICKY TOASTS**, you'll need to broil or pan-grill a heap of slender Italian bread slices—a large loaf of sourdough, ciabatta, or the like should do it—until a little charred in places. Rub the hot, crisp toast surfaces with a halved garlic clove, and drizzle with a little of your best olive oil. Pile up on a board beside the Strata.

CARAMEL-ALMOND PEARS

HANDS-ON TIME: 20 MINUTES

8 wooden sticks, cleaned
8 large pears, scrubbed
Flavorless oil
¾ cup toasted sliced almonds
2½ cups packed light brown sugar, preferably Muscovado sugar
¼ cup (½ stick) unsalted butter
1 tablespoon white wine vinegar
3 tablespoons golden syrup or light corn syrup

The ripeness of the pears is up to you; both crunchy and juicy-tender work beautifully with the caramel and nuts.

Stab a stick into the top (stem end) of each pear, then line them up, ready for dipping. Smear a little oil over a sheet of foil and use it to cover a baking sheet. Spread out the almonds on a small plate.

Put the sugar in a heavy-based pan with ½ cup cold water and heat gently, stirring until the sugar dissolves. Increase the heat and bring to a boil. Add the butter, vinegar, and syrup, but don't stir any more or the sugar might crystallize.

Keep the mixture simmering boldly until it reaches the "soft crack" stage, about 20 minutes. To test with a candy thermometer, it's when the caramel reaches about 280°F. To test freestyle, scoop out a tiny bit of caramel with a teaspoon and drop it into a glass of cold water. You will be able to pull it apart into hard but pliable threads between your fingers when the soft crack stage has been reached.

Remove the pan from the heat and, holding the sticks, quickly dip the pears into the caramel, turning to coat, then roll the bases in the sliced almonds. Let set on the oiled foil in a cool place (not the refrigerator) for at least 15 minutes before eating (eat them within a couple of hours or they'll become sticky).

AN ELEGANT PARTY FOR A WINTER'S NIGHT

Cumin-Spiced Lamb Skewers with a Fresh Chutney

Sweet Potato Samosas

Sticky Tamarind Chicken Wings

Rice Pudding Squares with Star Anise Plums

Orange-Blossom Mimosas

Light and Stormies

There's a vaguely Asian theme going on here, which seems appropriate for an elegant winter gathering. Assuming you'll have about 12 guests, the following menu will feed them well, although it will stretch to feed 18, or even 24 as long as there's plenty of wine. There are a few tips in the recipes on how to do this sneakily without anyone noticing.

CUMIN-SPICED LAMB SKEWERS WITH A FRESH CHUTNEY

HANDS-ON TIME: 20 MINUTES

FOR THE SKEWERS

2½ pounds boneless leg of lamb, cubed
2 teaspoons coriander seeds
1 tablespoon cumin seeds
3 fat garlic cloves, crushed
1 cup Greek yogurt
2 teaspoons brown sugar
2 tablespoons sunflower oil, plus more for the baking sheets
Small bunch of mint, leaves minced, plus more whole leaves for garnish
Salt and pepper

FOR THE FRESH CHUTNEY

2 large, ripe mangoes, peeled and finely diced
2 red chiles, minced
Finely grated zest and juice of 1 lime
2 teaspoons brown sugar

Stretch this to feed more by using larger cubes of lamb, removing them from their skewers once cooked, and piling up on plates with the chutney and an espresso cup of cocktail sticks alongside. This is stingier than serving a skewer each, but it will go further... Makes 24–26.

Put the lamb in a large mixing bowl. Toast the coriander and cumin seeds in a dry frying pan until fragrant. Tip into a pestle and mortar and crush roughly. Sprinkle the spices over the lamb along with the garlic, yogurt, sugar, oil, and two-thirds of the minced mint. Use your hands to work the flavorings into the meat Let marinate for a couple of hours, or overnight if you can.

Combine all the fresh chutney ingredients and stir in the remaining minced mint. Refrigerate until needed.

Before cooking, soak 24–36 wooden skewers in cold water for at least 30 minutes. This will prevent them from scorching under the heat.

Preheat the broiler. Season the lamb well and thread two or three cubes onto each skewer. Line the skewers up on lightly oiled baking sheets. Broil, about 4 inches from the heat, for about 6 minutes, turning the skewers over halfway through. Serve on warm platters, garnished with mint leaves and with the chutney in a bowl on the side.

SWEET POTATO SAMOSAS

HANDS-ON TIME: 30 MINUTES

- 2 tablespoons peanut oil
- 2 teaspoons mustard seeds
- 3 teaspoons cumin seeds
- 1 onion, finely chopped
- 1 tablespoon finely grated fresh ginger
- 2 garlic cloves, crushed
- 2 large sweet potatoes, peeled and diced into ½-inch cubes
- 2 green chiles, chopped (remove seeds, if you like)
- 2 cups frozen peas, thawed
- 2 teaspoons garam masala
- 3 tablespoons chopped cilantro
- Juice of ½ lemon
- Salt
- 12 sheets of phyllo pastry
- ½ cup butter (1 stick) or ghee, melted

A simple raita (an Indian side dish), made by stirring minced hothouse cucumber, red onion, and cilantro or mint into yogurt, would be lovely on the side. If you want spicier samosas, add more chiles, or use some that are very hot. Makes 24.

Heat the oil in a large pan. Add the mustard seeds with 1 teaspoon of the cumin seeds. When the mustard seeds start to pop, add the onion, ginger, and garlic and sauté for about 5 minutes. Throw in the sweet potato, chile, and 3 tablespoons water and cook, stirring from time to time, until the potato is just tender, 3–4 minutes longer.

Remove from the heat and stir in the peas, garam masala, cilantro, lemon juice, and salt to taste.

Preheat the oven to 375°F. Take one sheet of phyllo at a time (keep the rest covered with a damp dish towel to prevent it from drying out). Cut into two strips and brush them lightly with butter. Lay out one strip vertically on the work surface. Place a heaping tablespoon of the filling at the end nearest you. Lift up the bottom left-hand corner of the strip and fold it diagonally over the filling. Continue folding diagonally, alternating sides, to the end of the strip; you will have a triangular package. Brush with more butter and transfer to an oiled baking sheet. Repeat to make a total of 12 triangular packages.

Brush the samosas lightly again with butter and sprinkle with the remaining cumin seeds. Bake until lightly browned, about 15 minutes.

STICKY TAMARIND CHICKEN WINGS

HANDS-ON TIME: 15 MINUTES

- 2 ounces tamarind
- 2 tablespoons peanut oil
- 3 tablespoons honey
- 3 tablespoons dark brown sugar, preferably Muscovado sugar
- 2 tablespoons soy sauce
- Thumb-sized piece of fresh ginger, finely grated
- 2 fat garlic cloves, crushed
- 1 teaspoon dried chile flakes
- 24 small chicken wings
- Salt and pepper

In summer, try grilling these sweet-sour, caramelized wings outdoors. The glaze is also wonderful with pork and duck. If possible, use tamarind taken from a pliable block (the kind with flat seeds hidden among the dark brown pulp), rather than tamarind puree—with that none of the subtlety of the tangy fruit remains.

Place the tamarind in a bowl and pour in ½ cup boiling water. Mix with a fork and set aside for a few minutes. Strain the liquid, pressing the pulp in the strainer with the back of a spoon. Combine the tamarind liquid with the oil, honey, sugar, soy, ginger, garlic, and chile in a large bowl and mix well. Add the wings, stirring to coat thoroughly. Let marinate in a cool place for 30 minutes, or refrigerate overnight if you can.

Preheat the oven to 400°F. Season the wings and spread out on baking sheets in a single layer. Bake, turning once, until caramelized brown and sticky, 25–30 minutes. Serve hot, with plenty of paper napkins.

RICE PUDDING SQUARES WITH STAR ANISE PLUMS

HANDS-ON TIME: 30 MINUTES

2 heaping cups risotto rice
8 cups milk
2 cups sugar
1 large cinnamon stick
Salt
1¼ cups heavy cream
4 extra-large free-range eggs, beaten
2 free-range egg yolks
Finely grated zest of 1 orange
Star Anise Plums (see right), for serving

This recipe actually makes a dense rice-pudding cake that can be sliced neatly once chilled—a boon for portioning out at a party. Start this well in advance, even a couple of days ahead if you can.

The day (or even 2 days) before, combine the rice, milk, and sugar in a very large saucepan and add the cinnamon stick and a pinch of salt. Bring to a boil very slowly, stirring occasionally, then reduce the heat and simmer gently, stirring often, until the rice is cooked and most of the liquid has been absorbed, about 20 minutes.

Stir in the cream, then let cool for at least 2 hours, stirring occasionally to prevent a skin from forming. The rice pudding will thicken further as it cools.

Meanwhile, line an 11½ x 13½-inch baking pan with parchment paper. Preheat the oven to 325°F.

Add the eggs, yolks, and zest to the rice and mix well, fishing out the cinnamon stick as you do so. Pour into the prepared pan and smooth out evenly. Bake until golden, about 40 minutes. The rice cake will still be a bit wobbly in the middle. Let cool for a couple of hours, then refrigerate for 2–3 hours, or overnight if possible.

Unmold the cake onto a board. Peel off the lining paper and cut into 24 equal squares. Serve each piece in a small bowl, or on a saucer, with a Star Anise Plum half on top and some plum syrup spooned over the dessert.

To make **STAR ANISE PLUMS**, halve and pit 12 firm dark plums. Sprinkle the cut side of each half with a large pinch of sugar—I use Demerara. Place a large frying pan over medium heat. Add half the plums, cut sides down, to the pan and cook until just beginning to caramelize, 1–2 minutes. Remove to a plate and repeat with the remaining plums. Add 1¾ cups port or red wine to the pan along with 4 star anise flowers, 1 cup water and 1¼ cups Demerara sugar. Bring to a boil and simmer briskly until syrupy, about 15 minutes. Tip in the plums and warm through for a minute, being careful as you want to preserve their shape. Remove from the heat and squeeze in the juice of ½ orange. Serve warm or cold. The plums will actually be better, and the syrup more perfumed, if you can make them the day before. If plums aren't in season, the recipe will be just as delicious if you make a simple substitution of 24 whole, pitted prunes, such as Agen prunes from France. Dispense with the caramelizing and gently poach the prunes in the simmering star anise liquid for 10 minutes.

LIGHT AND STORMIES

HANDS-ON TIME: A COUPLE OF MINUTES

¼ cup light rum
About ½ cup non-alcoholic ginger beer, to taste
Ice and lime slices, for serving

I prefer a light rum here, because a very dark, spicy rum can clash with the ginger a little too much. These quantities will make two drinks.

Fill a couple of highball glasses with ice. Pour the rum and the ginger beer into each, using as much—or as little—ginger beer as you want. Serve the cocktails with a thin slice of lime on the side.

To make truly beautiful **ORANGE-BLOSSOM MIMOSAS**, pour enough chilled, freshly squeezed orange juice into champagne flutes to fill them by one-third. Add 1–2 drops of orange-blossom water to each glass (drop it in from a teaspoon; you only need a tiny hint so as not to overpower the fizz). Top with chilled champagne or other good sparkling wine and serve immediately.

LATE SPRING TEA PARTY FOR 12

Egg and Watercress Rolls

Garden Platter with Shrimp and Smoked Mayonnaise

Early Strawberry and Elderflower Cake

Macadamia-Honeycomb Ice Cream Cones

Lemon-Verbena Lemonade

This is tea, not lunch, so it features rather a lot of sweet food. Unless you're the Queen of England, I imagine you don't hold tea parties every day, so it is intended as a bit of an old-fashioned British treat. As usual, practically everything can be made or prepared well in advance, ready to carry outside to a big table in the garden.

EGG AND WATERCRESS ROLLS

HANDS-ON TIME: 15 MINUTES

5 free-range eggs
2 tablespoons soft unsalted butter, plus more for buttering the rolls
2 tablespoons milk
Salt and pepper
12 small, soft rolls, white or brown, split open
Watercress leaves, any coarse stems removed

I've been making egg sandwiches like this for more than 20 years and, although I'm fickle enough to neglect them for months—even years—whenever the need for an old-fashioned sandwich arises, this is what I want.

Cover the eggs (make sure they're not too fresh or they'll be hard to shell) with cold water and bring to a boil. Once boiling, set the timer and simmer for 5 minutes.

Refresh briefly under cold water, then peel. Put the warm eggs in a mixing bowl, add the butter and milk, and use a small knife to chop the eggs into small pieces. The residual heat will melt the butter. Season generously with salt and pepper. Divide among the buttered rolls and add a little watercress to each one.

For every enthusiast falling upon an egg sandwich with glee, there will be those who decline. This is merely the way of the world. The naysayers might be interested in some **OTHER GOOD SANDWICH IDEAS**, so I've listed a few below to get you thinking. Use whatever bread you prefer, but—in deference to the classy picnic—cut off the crusts and slice the filled sandwiches into triangles or fingers. Try these:

Soft goat cheese, tapenade, and basil ★ Finely sliced radish, hothouse cucumber, and salted butter ★ Blue brie, baby arugula, and ripe fig ★ Marinated artichoke hearts, fresh pesto, and buffalo mozzarella ★ Roast beef slices, crème fraîche, and horseradish ★ Prosciutto, tomato, avocado, and mayonnaise ★ Sliced sausage, basil leaves, and peperonata ★ Hot-smoked salmon and wasabi cream

Use a vegetable peeler to pare the zest from a couple of lemons in thick strips. Cut the lemons in half and squeeze out the juice. Combine the juice and zest in a large saucepan with about 30 lemon verbena leaves, 2½ cups sugar, and 4 cups water. Bring to a boil slowly, stirring to dissolve the sugar, and simmer gently for 5 minutes. Let cool, then strain the lemon verbena syrup into sterilized bottles (see page 89) and keep in the refrigerator for up to a month.

To make **LEMON-VERBENA LEMONADE**, pour a little lemon verbena syrup into each tall glass filled with ice and lemon slices. Dilute with sparkling water to taste. Add a shot of gin for those who give the nod.

OVENEX

GARDEN PLATTER WITH SHRIMP AND SMOKED MAYONNAISE

HANDS-ON TIME: 20 MINUTES

Sweet or sweet-hot paprika and smoked sea salt will donate an unusual smoky flavor to mayonnaise. You don't have to use the fancy salt, but I definitely recommend the smoked paprika. This mayonnaise is also good in an elegant smoked chicken and arugula sandwich.

FOR THE MAYONNAISE

3 extra-large, free-range egg yolks
Pinch of smoked sea salt (or plain flaked sea salt)
1 teaspoon sweet or sweet-hot smoked paprika, to taste
⅔ cup mild-flavored olive oil
1¼ cups peanut oil
Lemon juice, to taste

FOR THE REST

1½ pounds cooked, peeled (but tail-on) tiger shrimp
10 ounces baby bulb fennel, trimmed and halved from top to bottom
10 ounces baby carrots, scrubbed
7 ounces radishes, with leaves, washed
2 heads of baby romaine, leaves washed and separated
4 ounces Italian bread sticks (grissini)

It's easiest to make the mayonnaise in a food processor, but you can use a bowl and whisk (and a strong arm) instead. Briefly blend the yolks with the salt and paprika. With the machine running, start adding the olive oil, drop by drop. As the oil is incorporated you can increase the flow, but don't add it too fast or the mayonnaise could split. Start adding the peanut oil, gradually increasing the flow, blending until the mayonnaise is thick and shiny. If it does split, add another yolk and blend into the mixture, then continue adding the oil. Brighten the seasoning with lemon juice and more paprika, if you want. Check the seasoning and whisk in a little warm water if too thick.

Pile the shrimp into a couple of deep bowls and set in a large, wide, shallow bowl filled with ice. Spoon the mayonnaise into three or four small pots and nestle into the ice beside the shrimp. Pile the vegetables prettily on a platter and the lettuce on a plate, and stand the bread sticks in a jar or tall glass alongside. All is ready.

EARLY STRAWBERRY AND ELDERFLOWER CAKE

HANDS-ON TIME: 25 MINUTES

The fragrance of the flowers of the elder tree is difficult to capture in a cake batter; their perfume becomes elusive after a stint in the oven. After much experimentation, the best way seems to be through including the fresh or dried blossoms in the batter, then giving the warm cake a generous soaking in elderflower syrup afterward. Frothy elderberry flowers are only in season in early summer. If you can get fresh blossoms, shake them well to dislodge any little bugs before decorating the cake.

FOR THE CAKE

1 cup (2 sticks) unsalted butter, very soft
1 cup + 2 tablespoons sugar
4 free-range eggs, lightly beaten
1⅔ cups self-rising flour
½ teaspoon baking powder
2 tablespoons ground almonds
1 tablespoon fresh or dried elderberry flowers (optional)
¼ cup milk
Finely grated zest of 1 lemon

FOR THE SYRUP

½ cup Elderflower Syrup (see page 183)
Finely grated zest and juice of ½ lemon
1 tablespoon Demerara sugar

Preheat the oven to 350°F. Line the bottom and sides of a deep 9-inch springform cake pan with parchment paper. Cream the butter and sugar together until light and fluffy. Gradually add the eggs as you continue to beat, adding a spoonful of flour to stabilize the mixture if it starts to curdle (though that doesn't matter too much). Sift in the flour and baking powder and add the ground almonds, elderflowers (if using), milk, and zest. Fold in with a large metal spoon or a spatula. Scrape into the pan and level the surface. Bake until risen and golden brown, 40–45 minutes. Loosely cover the cake with a layer of parchment paper or foil if it is browning too much.

Meanwhile, combine the elderflower syrup, lemon zest and juice, and Demerara in a small pitcher. The sugar won't dissolve: it will provide a crunch on top of the cake.

Let the cake cool in the pan for 5 minutes, then use a skewer to puncture the cake several times. Pour the syrup over the top. Let the cake cool completely in the pan.

Hull one-third of the strawberries and use a fork to crush with the sugar and 1 tablespoon of the elderflower syrup. Either leave as is or pass the mixture through a strainer to remove the strawberry seeds and create a smooth puree.

Just before serving, hull the remaining strawberries and halve any large ones. Put into a bowl. Whip the cream with the remaining 2 tablespoons syrup until it just holds a floppy shape. Marble the strawberry puree through the cream, being careful not to over-mix so you keep the rippled effect. Pile into a bowl. Decorate the top of the cake with a few elderberry flowerheads, if you have them.

Serve each slice with the hulled strawberries and marbled strawberry cream.

NOTE: Not widely grown in the U.S., elderberries are available online through some herb distributors.

FOR THE STRAWBERRY CREAM

1½ pounds early strawberries
2 tablespoons sugar
3 tablespoons Elderflower Syrup (see page 183)
2 cups heavy cream
Fresh elderberry flowerheads, for garnish (optional)

MACADAMIA–HONEYCOMB ICE CREAM CONES

HANDS-ON TIME: 40 MINUTES

FOR THE HONEYCOMB
- 2 tablespoons white wine vinegar
- ⅔ cup golden syrup or light corn syrup
- 1½ cups sugar
- 1½ teaspoons baking soda

FOR THE ICE CREAM
- 1 cup macadamia nuts
- 2½ cups heavy cream
- 1 14-ounce can sweetened condensed milk

It must be the way the caramel foams scarily when you add the soda that makes any recipe for honeycomb seem pure alchemy—kids love helping to make it. When stirred into this ridiculously easy ice cream base, the honeycomb pieces turn to dreamy, liquid caramel, with just a hint of residual crunch at the center. If you have an ice cream machine, and a favorite vanilla ice cream recipe, you can make that instead. Just keep it on the less-sweet side because of all the honeycomb and nuts you'll be stirring in. As for the cones, although the version here is very simple and can be made a day in advance, they are there to gild the lily, so use bought ice cream cones instead if you'd prefer.

Start with the honeycomb, up to 3 days in advance. Line a large baking sheet with parchment paper. Heat the vinegar, syrup, and sugar together gently until the sugar dissolves completely. Increase the heat and boil, without stirring, until the caramel turns a dark amber color. Remove from the heat and sift the baking soda into the caramel. Quickly stir it in, then pour the foaming mixture into the prepared pan. Let cool and harden, then break or crush into small pieces.

To make the ice cream, preheat the oven to 350°F. Spread the nuts on a baking sheet and toast in the oven until pale golden, 6–8 minutes, shaking them over halfway through. Watch carefully because macadamias burn frustratingly easily. Let cool and chop roughly.

Whip the cream until soft peaks form, then add the condensed milk and whip again until the mixture is thick but not stiff. Reserve a couple of tablespoons of the chopped nuts and fold the rest into the cream mixture along with two-thirds of the honeycomb. Scrape into a large freezer container, cover, and freeze for at least 4 hours, or preferably overnight. Keep the remaining honeycomb and nuts for serving.

To make the ice cream cones, form a couple of cone-shaped molds out of double layers of foil and lightly butter the outside of each. Each should be about 5½ inches long and wide enough to hold a scoop of ice cream. Make sure the oven is heated to 350°F and line a large baking sheet with parchment paper.

Gently heat the sugar, syrup, and butter in a pan until the sugar has dissolved. Remove from the heat and stir in the flour. Drop a tablespoon of the batter onto the lined baking sheet to form a disk. Repeat to make two or three disks in total. Make sure they are spaced well apart, because they will spread as they heat up. Bake until dark golden, about 6 minutes.

Remove from the oven and let settle for half a minute, then lift up a warm disk with a spatula and quickly curl it around a cone mold with your hands, pinching the pointed end to seal. Let set for a minute, then carefully unmold and transfer to a wire rack. Repeat until all the batter is used. If the baked disks cool too much to be pliable, return them to the oven for a minute to soften up. This will make at least 12 cones. Keep in an airtight container for up to a day.

To serve, carefully set a scoop of ice cream in each cone and sprinkle with the reserved crushed honeycomb and macadamias. The trick is to finish eating the ice cream before it melts through the cones.

FOR THE CONES

7 tablespoons unsalted butter, plus more for the molds
½ cup packed light brown sugar
3 heaping tablespoons golden syrup or light corn syrup
½ cup + 1 tablespoon all-purpose flour, sifted

GLAZED CARROT BIRTHDAY CAKE

SERVES 10-12
HANDS-ON TIME: 30 MINUTES

This spicy, nutty carrot cake can rival the best of them in the indulgence stakes and makes a gorgeous dessert or grown-up birthday cake. The caramel and mascarpone glaze is a fancy variation on cream cheese frosting.

FOR THE CAKE
1⅔ cups self-rising flour
1 teaspoon baking powder
1 teaspoon baking soda
½ teaspoon salt
2 teaspoons ground cinnamon
1 teaspoon ground ginger
1½ cups packed light brown sugar
1 cup vegetable oil or very mild olive oil
4 free-range eggs
2 cups finely grated carrots
1 cup chopped pecans or walnuts
4 balls preserved ginger in syrup, finely chopped, plus ¼ cup syrup

FOR THE FILLING
½ cup mascarpone
½ cup fromage blanc
2 tablespoons sugar

FOR THE GLAZE
½ cup + 2 tablespoons sugar
½ cup mascarpone
½ teaspoon ground cinnamon
1 tablespoon lemon juice
½ cup finely chopped pecans or walnuts

Line the bottom and sides of two 9-inch round cake pans with parchment paper. Preheat the oven to 350°F. Sift the dry ingredients, except the brown sugar, into a large bowl. In another bowl, beat the sugar, oil, and eggs together, then stir in the carrots, nuts, ginger, and ginger syrup. Pour this into the dry ingredients and mix well. Divide between the pans. Bake until risen and springy to the touch, about 25 minutes. Let cool for 5 minutes, then unmold onto a wire rack to cool completely.

To make the filling, briefly beat the mascarpone, fromage blanc, and sugar together. Don't overbeat, because the mascarpone can split or become runny. Set one cake layer on a serving plate and spread thickly with the filling. Set the other cake layer on top.

Gently heat the sugar with 3 tablespoons water in a heavy-based saucepan, stirring until the sugar dissolves. Increase the heat and boil until the syrup turns to golden caramel. Remove from the heat and add 2 tablespoons water; the caramel will sputter. Use a wire whisk to stir in the mascarpone, cinnamon, and lemon juice until smooth. Let cool and thicken for a minute or so, then pour the glaze over the top of the cake, letting it run down the sides in rivulets. Scatter the nuts over the top.

HOT SUMMER BARBECUE FOR SIX

Skirt Steaks with Red Chimichurri Sauce, Tortillas, and Sour Cream

Charred Corn Salsa

Avocado Salsa

Best Brownies

As is usually the case, the barbecue will imbue these recipes with a certain smoky something (apart from the brownies, that is), but they can all be cooked indoors under the broiler or on a grill pan instead. The Argentine-style marinade for the beef is on the feisty side of hot, so tone down the cayenne if you prefer. The marinade can be kept in a covered jar in the refrigerator for a few weeks, ready to pep up chicken, lamb, pork, or shrimp as a marinade, or grilled vegetables as a sauce.

SKIRT STEAKS WITH RED CHIMICHURRI SAUCE, TORTILLAS, AND SOUR CREAM

HANDS-ON TIME: 25 MINUTES

FOR THE MARINADE
7 tablespoons sherry vinegar
3 tablespoons extra-virgin olive oil
3 fat garlic cloves, minced
2 fresh bay leaves, torn
1½ teaspoons cumin seeds, toasted and ground
1 tablespoon hot paprika
½ teaspoon cayenne pepper
1 teaspoon coarsely ground black pepper
Salt

FOR THE STEAKS
6 skirt steaks (about 7 ounces each)
12 soft corn or flour tortillas

FOR SERVING
2 cups sour cream
Salad leaves
Charred Corn Salsa and Avocado Salsa (see right)

Wonderfully tender and flavorsome skirt steak is traditionally used for fajitas. Not being dense in texture, the meat absorb the punchy flavors of a marinade, such as this one. Skirt is best given a long, slow braising, or, as here, fast grilling over charcoal for the juiciest steak.

Combine all the marinade ingredients and pour half into a non-reactive dish. Add the steaks and let marinate for 1 hour. Reserve the remaining marinade (this is the chimichurri sauce). Meanwhile, prepare the fire in the barbecue. Wrap the tortillas thickly in foil and place on a not-so-hot area of the grill to warm through.

Lift the steaks from the marinade, season with salt, and place on the grill. Sear for about 2 minutes on each side for rare, 3 minutes on each side for medium-rare, or to the desired degree of doneness. (These are only guideline times because the steaks will vary in thickness.) Remove the cooked steaks to a warmed plate and let them rest for 5 minutes before cutting.

Slice the steaks across the grain and serve with the warm tortillas, sour cream, salad, and salsas, plus the reserved chimichurri sauce to spoon over the steak and salad.

CHARRED CORN SALSA

HANDS-ON TIME: 15 MINUTES

4 large ears of corn, shucked
2 green chiles, deseeded and minced
1 14-ounce can black beans, rinsed and drained
Juice of ½ lime
1 teaspoon brown sugar
Small handful of cilantro leaves, chopped
Salt

Fried this way, without any oil, corn kernels become deliciously charred and take on a chewy nuttiness. They make a fine salsa paired with black beans and perked up with a touch of lime and cilantro.

Using a small, sharp knife, cut the kernels from the cobs. Heat a large frying pan on the grill, or over medium-high heat, and add the corn kernels along with the chiles. Dry-fry, stirring often, until the kernels are browned, about 10 minutes. Let cool.

Once cooled, combine with the beans in a serving bowl. Add the lime juice, sugar, cilantro, and salt to taste. Stir well and serve.

To make an **AVOCADO SALSA** with smoky depth, place a doubled sheet of foil on the grill and on this arrange 4 small plum (Roma) tomatoes, 1 fresh red jalapeño chile, and 3 unpeeled garlic cloves. (You can also use a smoking hot grill pan.) Cook, turning with tongs every now and then, until the tomatoes are blackened and blistered all over and the chile and garlic are soft, about 10 minutes. Let cool. Halve and pit 3 large avocados and mash the flesh coarsely. Squeeze the juice of ½ lime over the avocado and stir in ½ finely chopped red onion. Remove the stem and seeds from the chile, and peel the skins from the garlic and tomatoes. Crush the garlic and chile using a pestle and mortar with a large pinch of flaked sea salt; add the peeled tomatoes, with any of their collected juices, and pound to a rough paste. (Or use a food processor to pulse the garlic, chile, salt, and tomatoes until coarse-fine.) Mix into the avocado mixture with a small handful of chopped cilantro leaves to finish.

BEST BROWNIES

HANDS-ON TIME: 20 MINUTES

- 10 ounces bittersweet chocolate, broken into pieces
- 1 cup (2 sticks) unsalted butter
- 4 extra-large free-range eggs
- 1 cup granulated sugar
- ¾ cup packed light brown sugar
- 1 teaspoon vanilla extract
- Scant 1 cup all-purpose flour
- ½ teaspoon baking powder
- ½ teaspoon salt
- 3½ tablespoons unsweetened cocoa powder

These brownies have been honed to perfection over many years and I've never known anyone to not ask for the recipe. I'm not a fan of nuts in my brownies, but don't let that stop you throwing in a handful of chopped walnuts or pecans. This makes 16 bars or 32 smaller squares.

Line a 9 x 13-inch pan, at least 2 inches deep, with parchment paper. Preheat the oven to 375°F. Melt two-thirds of the chocolate with the butter in a pan over low heat (or in a bowl set over a pan of simmering water, or in the microwave). Stir occasionally, until smooth. Let cool. Chop the remaining chocolate.

Beat the eggs, sugars, and vanilla together for a couple of minutes, to give a light texture. Sift in the flour, baking powder, salt, and cocoa powder, then pour in the melted chocolate mixture. Beat briefly to combine, then stir in the chopped chocolate. Scrape into the pan

Reduce the oven temperature to 350°F and bake until set around the edges and almost firm in the middle, 35–40 minutes. Let cool in the pan for at least 15 minutes, then unmold carefully and cut into bars or squares. The brownies will keep in an airtight container for up to 4 days.

ELDERFLOWER SYRUP

MAKES THREE 1-PINT BOTTLES
HANDS-ON TIME: 20 MINUTES

- 25 large, fresh elderberry flowerheads
- 2 lemons
- 1 small orange
- 10 cups sugar
- 2½ ounces citric acid

I guarantee you'll use this beautifully perfumed syrup often. It's especially useful for non-alcoholic cocktails, diluted with sparkling water, served in tumblers with ice cubes and lemon slices. Or add generously to creamy puddings, ice creams, and gelatin molds to scent them with summer. Gather the creamy-white blossoms in June. Health food stores often carry citric acid.

Shake the flowerheads to remove any bugs that might be lurking. Place the flowerheads in a large bowl. Pare the zest from the citrus fruits using a vegetable peeler, then thinly slice the fruits, pith and all. Add to the bowl.

Heat the sugar with 4 cups of water in a large pan until the sugar has dissolved. Bring gently to a boil, then remove from the heat and add the citric acid. Pour into the bowl of blossoms and fruit. Cover with a saucepan lid and leave in a cool place for a day or two (no longer or the mixture may start to ferment).

Strain the syrup through a sieve, then through a layer of cheesecloth. Divide among sterilized bottles (see page 89), seal, and keep in a cool, dark cupboard for up to 3 months. Once opened, keep in the refrigerator.

NOTE: Not widely grown in the U.S., elderberries are available online through some herb distributors.

QUICK PARTY FOOD IDEAS

At a casual party you don't have to serve food conventionally. Rather than preparing potatoes and side dishes, offer **ROAST PORK ROLLS**. Set up a table with a stack of plates and napkins and add warmed, crusty bread rolls, plenty of applesauce, and a platter of shredded or pulled, herb-scented roast pork. It's easy for everyone to put together their own roll. This needs nothing more than a salad on the side.

The same self-service treatment works well for a warmed loaf of bread (or a selection of crackers), a **REALLY BEAUTIFUL WHOLE CHEESE**, and a jar of fig preserves. Arrange these on a wooden board with suitable knives—and a spoon for the preserves—and some small plates alongside. An Asian salad of finely shredded vegetables and rice noodles will go perfectly with the cheese and won't wilt on standing.

SCALLOPS are self-portioning wonders, especially if you can serve them in their cleaned half-shells. Simmer peeled and chopped parsnips in seasoned milk until tender, then blend with butter, nutmeg, and enough of the milk to make a puree; keep warm. Fry some chunky cubes of pancetta in olive oil until browned and crisp, then scoop out to drain on paper towels. Pat sea scallops dry (halve them horizontally if they are big), season with salt, pepper, and thyme leaves, and fry briefly in the pancetta fat until crusty on the outside and tender within. Return the pancetta to the pan, just to warm through. Serve each seared scallop on the half-shell (or in a little ramekin) with a spoonful of parsnip puree, a cube or two of pancetta, and a teaspoon for eating.

Perfect a couple of **POPULAR COCKTAILS**. Start with the simplest classics: they'll always be appreciated. But be sure to use the best ingredients. A beautifully made gin and tonic will be enjoyed at most parties—made with good gin, fresh lime, and old-fashioned tonic water.

POPSICLES are right up there in the childhood nostalgia stakes, but bring them right up to date. Silicone ice cube trays make brilliant molds for 21st-century ice treats. Freeze highly flavored and unchurned granitas, sorbets, ice creams, fruit compotes, and even cocktails (go easy on the booze, because too much alcohol will prevent the mixture from freezing solid) in ice cube trays; while the mix is still a little slushy, stand a wooden stick in each one. The possibilities for new-fangled flavors are endless: try pear and rosemary sorbet; blueberry yogurt ice; mojito; passion fruit and coconut ice cream; Vietnamese coffee granita...

◇◇

I usually don't like to tweak traditional recipes too much (I have fond memories of enjoying a more authentic version of these in Macau), but frozen butter puff pastry and an easy custard will make delectable **PORTUGUESE-STYLE CUSTARD TARTS**. To make 24 tarts, preheat the oven to 400°F. Roll up a sheet of puff pastry (about 10 ounces) to form a tight cylinder. Slice across into 24 rounds; each should be about ½ inch wide. Roll each of these pieces out a little thinner, and use to line the cups of two lightly buttered 12-cup muffin pans. If the edges are a little raggedy, that's fine. Whisk 5 free-range egg yolks with 1 whole egg, 1 cup sugar, and ¼ cup cornstarch. Gradually whisk in 1¾ cups each cream and milk. Pour into a pan and stir over medium heat until the mixture boils and thickens. Add the seeds from a vanilla bean, or a dusting of ground cinnamon. Cover the surface with plastic wrap to prevent a skin from forming, then let cool. Divide the cooled custard among the pastry shells. Bake until browned, about 25 minutes. Cool in the pans for a few minutes, then transfer the tarts to wire racks to cool completely.

Warm 12 small bowls, ready to fill with a classic **EGG-FRIED RICE**. Stir-fry 1 pound raw, peeled shrimp in peanut oil in a wok until pink; remove. Add 2 beaten free-range eggs, swirling until cooked to an omelet. Roughly chop the shrimp and cut the omelet into strips. Increase the heat, add more oil, and fry chopped garlic and fresh ginger for a few seconds before stirring in 3 heaping cups cold, cooked jasmine or basmati rice. Heat through. Stir in the shrimp and season with oyster sauce, soy sauce, sugar, salt, and toasted sesame oil. Fold in the omelet with a handful of shredded scallions. Divide among the bowls. Stick a fork (this is not the time for chopsticks: there'll be rice all over the floor) into each and provide a bottle of chile sauce.

Slowly fry a finely sliced onion until golden, then pep up with a sprinkle of cumin seeds, ground cinnamon, paprika, and a few minced dates. Remove from the heat and add 1 pound lean ground lamb, 3 tablespoons soft bread crumbs, 1 beaten free-range egg, and some chopped mint. Halve 12 sheets of phyllo pastry crosswise and brush with melted butter. Fold a piece of phyllo in half. Pile a heaping tablespoon of lamb filling at one end, tuck in the edges, and roll up to form a chubby cigar. Seal with beaten egg and brush with more butter. Repeat to make 24. Bake at 400°F until golden, about 20 minutes. Stir 1 tablespoon harissa into some Greek yogurt, sharpen with lemon, and serve in a bowl beside a pile of hot **LAMB CIGARS**.